A CRUCIBLE OF FIRE

THE BATTLE OF LUNDY'S LANE, JULY 25, 1814

UPPER CANADA PRESERVED
WAR OF 1812

A CRUCIBLE OF FIRE
THE BATTLE OF LUNDY'S LANE, JULY 25, 1814

RICHARD FELTOE

DUNDURN
TORONTO

Editor: Allison Hirst
Design: Jennifer Scott
Printer: Webcom

Library and Archives Canada Cataloguing in Publication

Feltoe, Richard, 1954-, author
　　A crucible of fire : the Battle of Lundy's Lane, July 25, 1814 / Richard Feltoe.

(Upper Canada preserved War of 1812)
Includes bibliographical references and index.
Issued in print and electronic formats.
ISBN 978-1-4597-2212-5 (pbk.).--ISBN 978-1-4597-2213-2 (pdf).-- ISBN 978-1-4597-2214-9 (epub)

1. Lundy's Lane, Battle of, Ont., 1814. 2. Lundy's Lane, Battle of, Ont., 1814--Sources. I. Title. II. Series: Feltoe, Richard, 1954- . Upper Canada preserved War of 1812.

FC446.L8F44 2014　　　　　971.03'4　　　　C2013-908372-3　　　　C2013-908373-1

1　2　3　4　5　　　18　17　16　15　14

We acknowledge the support of the Canada Council for the Arts and the Ontario Arts Council for our publishing program. We also acknowledge the financial support of the Government of Canada through the Canada Book Fund and Livres Canada Books, and the Government of Ontario through the Ontario Book Publishing Tax Credit and the Ontario Media Development Corporation.

Visit us at
Dundurn.com | @dundurnpress | Facebook.com/dundurnpress | Pinterest.com/dundurnpress

Dundurn	Gazelle Book Services Limited	Dundurn
3 Church Street, Suite 500	White Cross Mills	2250 Military Road
Toronto, Ontario, Canada	High Town, Lancaster, England	Tonawanda, NY
M5E 1M2	LA1 4XS	U.S.A. 14150

TABLE OF CONTENTS

ACKNOWLEDGEMENTS

To completely misquote Prime Minister Winston Churchill, "Never has so much been owed by one to so many." As such, as we move to book five of this series, the list of those deserving of thanks for their contributions and support grows ever longer. Unfortunately, there is never enough space within these published pages to adequately recognize each and every individual by name, and for this I wholeheartedly apologize. However, as in the past, certain people and organizations have made exceptional efforts on my behalf to support this project and it would be remiss of me not to at least recognize them.

First and foremost would be my wife, Diane, who is my "front line" in the management of all the business end of things, and who, by some gracious miracle, continues to tolerate and accept my ongoing absences and hermit-like seclusions when I'm upstairs in the "computer" room, writing for hours on end.

Second, my grateful thanks go to my friend and fellow historian on the American side of the Niagara River, Pat Kavanagh, who freely and without hesitation gave me unrestricted access to his vast resource collection of American records, official documents, and personal letters on the war. Without his aid and resources, this work could definitely not have been created.

Next would be to credit the leadership and example provided by one of Canada's leading historians, Donald Graves, in showing me the value of dedicated scholarship and for producing quality published works about our nation's heritage and history that I could refer to as a comparison and to cross-check the details and references that I have accumulated in my own research.

Beyond that come a host of dedicated staff members of the numerous museums, archives, and libraries that I visited to undertake the research for this work and who cheerfully assisted me in my searches to bring this work to fruition.

Nor can I fail to acknowledge the continued guidance and support provided by both my former editor, Cheryl Hawley, and my new guide to the mysteries (and frustrations) of editing, Allison Hirst, as well as my talented designer, Jennifer Scott, all backed by the extensive creative team at Dundurn in turning this idea into a reality.

Penultimately, I wish to thank Barry Penhale and Jane Gibson of Natural Heritage publications and my friend Karen who sadly passed away. These three collectively put my feet on the path that allowed me to become an author.

Finally, I want to go on record in expressing my deepest gratitude and thanks to all my readers, who have supported me by buying my books, overwhelmed me by their kind reviews and compliments on the series so far, and provided suggestions for ensuring the remaining parts maintain their deservedly high expectations.

PREFACE

VARIATIONS

In writing a military history and using original quotes, every author on this subject has to deal with a certain set of problems in presenting their material. First, there is the fact that in the original documents one is dealing with historical personalities, each with varied levels of education and skills of writing and spelling, not all of which correspond to our own modern forms. Second, there are the inevitable references to official military formations, regimental affiliations, ranks and appointments, battlefield tactics and manoeuvres, et cetera that can sometimes appear alien to a modern reader not familiar with the subject. Third, there is the reality that place names have sometimes changed entirely or have gained different spellings over the years.

To address these points, this author has chosen to adopt the following position in the presentation of his accumulated materials.

On the matter of varied spellings in quotes, the material has been repeatedly checked to ensure its accuracy and is presented just as I found it in the original documents. I have therefore not included the highly distracting term *sic* after each variant word as it drives me to distraction when I see it used in other works and in my opinion effectively destroys the integrity and meaning of the quote to me as a reader. As I see it in reading works of this kind, either I trust that the author did his job properly and the quote is accurate, or I don't and I go and look it up for myself if I'm so inclined.

On the second point, while generally recognized military terms are presented as is, some of the more archaic or jargon-type words are either followed by a modern equivalent. In a similar manner, maintaining the differential identification of military units from the two principal combatant nations (when both used a system of numbers to designate their regiments) has forced many modern writers to develop a system that will maintain a clear identity for their readers. I have adopted this convention and within this work British regimental numbers are shown as numerals (41st Regiment, 89th Regiment) and where required with their subsidiary titles (1st [Royal Scots] Regiment, 8th [King's] Regiment), whilst the American regiments are expressed as words (First Regiment, Twenty-Fifth Regiment).

Finally, where place names appear under a number of variants (e.g. Sackett's Harbour, Sacket's Harbour, Sakets Harbor, or Sacket's Harbor), I have adopted a single format for each case, based upon a judgment of what I felt was the predominant version used at the time. Where names have changed entirely, or would cause needless confusion (Newark becoming Niagara and currently Niagara-on-the-Lake), I have generally gone with what would clarify the location and simplify identification overall or included a reference to the modern name (Crossroads becoming Virgil.)

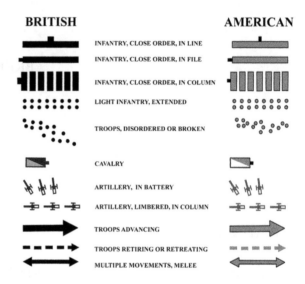

BRITISH		AMERICAN
	INFANTRY, CLOSE ORDER, IN LINE	
	INFANTRY, CLOSE ORDER, IN FILE	
	INFANTRY, CLOSE ORDER, IN COLUMN	
	LIGHT INFANTRY, EXTENDED	
	TROOPS, DISORDERED OR BROKEN	
	CAVALRY	
	ARTILLERY, IN BATTERY	
	ARTILLERY, LIMBERED, IN COLUMN	
	TROOPS ADVANCING	
	TROOPS RETIRING OR RETREATING	
	MULTIPLE MOVEMENTS, MELEE	

CHAPTER 1

Introduction

By July 1814, the fate of Upper Canada hung in the balance. Following a declaration of war in June 1812 and some twenty-five months of frustrating and unsuccessful attempts to conquer and occupy the British colonies in North America, the United States army of the "Left Division," under the overall command of Major General Jacob Brown, crossed the southern extremity of the Niagara River to Fort Erie on Sunday, July 3, 1814, in order to begin yet another invasion attempt.

Composed of an estimated five thousand troops and formed into three brigades,[*1] (see chart on page 25) the core of this army represented the most highly trained and disciplined military force the United States had yet fielded against the British army, its Canadian militias, and British Native allies (hereafter British or allied forces). Two days later, this American army took on and decisively defeated a strong allied force at the Battle of Chippawa, just upriver from the Great Falls of Niagara. This victory opened the way to a possible routing of the entire British military stationed on the Niagara Peninsula. When coupled with America's absolute naval control of Lake Erie (already achieved) and military occupation of the Detroit frontier and parts of western Upper Canada, it created the very real possibility that British power in Upper Canada was about to come to an end.

The story of the formation of that American army and its initial campaign victories at Fort Erie and the Battle of Chippawa are detailed in *The Tide of War*, the fourth book in this series, Upper Canada Preserved, War of 1812. However, for those who have not read that work, the following

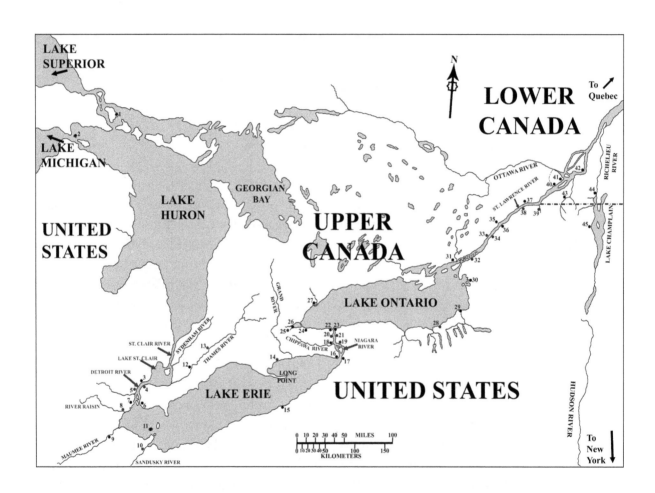

The "Northern Frontier" of the War of 1812–1815
(Modern Name)   [Fortifications]

1. St. Joseph Island [Fort St. Joseph]
2. Michilimackinac Island (Mackinac) [Fort Mackinac/Fort Michilimackinac]
3. Detroit [Fort Detroit]
4. Sandwich (Windsor)
5. Monguagon/ Maguaga
6. Amherstburg (Malden) [Fort Amherstburg]
7. Brownstown
8. Frenchtown
9. Perrysburg [Fort Meigs]
10. [Fort Stephenson]
11. Put-in-Bay
12. Moravianstown
13. Longwoods
14. Port Dover
15. Presque Isle (Erie, PA)
16. Fort Erie [Fort Erie]
17. Buffalo and Black Rock
18. Chippawa
19. [Fort Schlosser]
20. Queenston
21. Lewiston
22. Newark (Niagara-on-the-Lake) [Fort George, Fort Mississauga]
23. [Fort Niagara]
24. Stoney Creek
25. Ancaster
26. Burlington Heights (Hamilton, ON)
27. York (Toronto) [Fort York]
28. Sodus
29. Oswego [Fort Oswego]
30. Sackets Harbor [Fort Tompkins, Fort Volunteer, Fort Pike]
31. Kingston [Fort Frederick, Fort Henry]
32. French Creek
33. Elizabethtown/ Brockville (1813)
34. Morrisburg
35. Prescott [Fort Wellington]
36. Ogdensburg
37. Crysler's Farm
38. Hamilton (Waddington, NY)
39. French Mills
40. Coteau-du-Lac
41. Cedars
42. Montreal
43. Châteauguay
44. Île aux Noix
45. Plattsburg

synopsis of events that precede the beginning of this publication may prove helpful.

TIMELINE

- *April 14, 1814:* An American force, under the overall command of Major General Jacob Brown arrives at Buffalo, on the Niagara frontier, with orders to prepare and train for a springtime invasion of Upper Canada. In response, General Brown proposes that the major thrust of this invasion should take advantage of the American naval superiority on Lake Erie to transport and land a force of troops at Long Point, while a second, smaller force would threaten to make an invasion on the Niagara frontier, fixing the bulk of the enemy troops in place there. From Long Point, the landed troops would make a forced march on and capture Burlington Heights, thus cutting off the bulk of the British forces on the Niagara frontier from reinforcement or supply by land. At the same time, an American naval force would sail from Sackets Harbor and take control of Lake Ontario, preventing the British from using its fleet at Kingston to provide support by water to the Niagara frontier. After rendezvousing with Brown's army

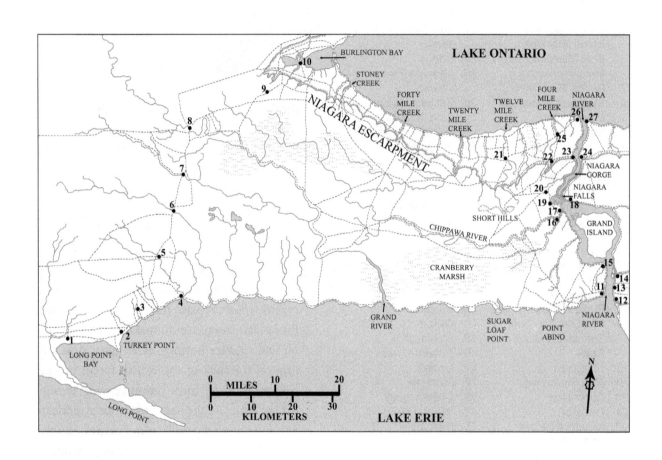

THE NIAGARA FRONTIER

Locations along the proposed American attack route from Long Point to Burlington Heights

1. Long Point (Port Rowan area)
2. Turkey Point
3. Dover (Port Dover)
4. Nanticoke
5. Union Mills (Simcoe)
6. Sovereign's Mills (Waterford)
7. Malcolm's Mill (Oakland)
8. Brantford
9. Ancaster
10. Burlington Heights

Locations along the actual American invasion route following the Niagara River

11. Fort Erie
12. Buffalo
13. Black Rock
14. Scajaquada Creek Navy Yard
15. Frenchman's Creek
16. Weishoun's Point
17. Chippawa Fortifications
18. Fort Schlosser
19. Bridgewater
20. Lundy's Lane/Portage Road crossroad
21. Shipman's Corners (St. Catharines)
22. St. Davids
23. Queenston
24. Lewiston
25. Crossroads (Virgil)
26. Fort Mississauga/Newark(Niagara-on-the-Lake)/ Fort George
27. Fort Niagara

and bringing it reinforcements and supplies, the fleet would maintain its blockade while Brown's forces would compel the enemy to fight or surrender on advantageous American terms. With this goal achieved, the Americans would control the bulk of Upper Canada and could then move in concert to take York (Toronto) and then Kingston.

- *April 21:* When Brown leaves to return to supervise the defence of Sackets Harbor, the training regimen and command of the army at Buffalo is assumed by Brigadier General Winfield Scott.
- *April–June:* Training of the Left Division continues.
- *May:* At Sackets Harbor, Major General Brown and Commodore Isaac Chauncey hold talks about the upcoming campaign on the Niagara frontier. Following these discussions, General Brown concludes he has a firm commitment and agreement from Commodore Chauncey to support Brown's army by transporting men, weapons, and supplies as required. Consequently, he bases his entire plan and subsequent campaign upon this premise. However, Commodore Chauncey's understanding is that he has made no such commitment and that his first priority is to oppose and defeat the British fleet under Sir James Yeo and not be a subservient transport to Brown's army.

- *May 14–16:* American forces at Presque Isle (Erie, Pennsylvania) make a series of amphibious landings and raids along the Upper Canada shoreline of Lake Erie between Dover Mills and Long Point. Backed by the firepower of their ships, superiority of numbers, and the fact that the local defence forces are unable to concentrate sufficient troops to oppose the invaders, the Americans are able to loot and destroy several communities, including Patterson's Creek (Lynn River), Charlotteville (Turkey Point), Dover Mills, Finch's Mills, Long Point, and Port Dover.

- *June:* The U.S. secretary of war, John Armstrong, responds to Brown's invasion proposals by claiming to support the initiative in principal. However, in practical terms, he strips Brown of the vital component of support of the bulk of the American Lake Erie fleet, as well as substantial numbers of troops, in order to mount an expedition to recapture the garrison post at Michilimackinac (Mackinac) at the north end of Lake Huron. Without this transport and supply component, Brown feels the mounting of an invasion via Long Point is impossible, leaving him with no option but to use his limited resources of boat transport to mount his invasion entirely across the Niagara River and through the Niagara River corridor.

Some of the Personalities of the War of 1812–1815
(Facing page: left to right)

Top Row:
Sir George Prevost (commander in chief, British Forces and governor general, British North America). S.W. Reynolds, artist, date unknown. *Library and Archives Canada, C-19123.*
Lieutenant General Gordon Drummond. G.T. Berthon, artist, circa 1882. *Archives of Ontario, Acc. 693127.*
Sir James Yeo (British senior naval commander, "Great Lakes"). *From* Pictorial Field Book of the War of 1812.

Middle Row:
James Madison (U.S. president). *Courtesy of the Buffalo and Erie County Historical Society Research Library, Buffalo, New York.*
John Armstrong (U.S. secretary of war). *Courtesy of the Buffalo and Erie County Historical Society Research Library, Buffalo, New York.*
Commodore Isaac Chauncey (U.S. naval commander, "Northern frontier"). *Library and Archives Canada, C-010926.*

Bottom Row:
Major General Jacob Brown. Attributed to J. Wood, engraver. *Courtesy of the Buffalo and Erie County Historical Society Research Library, Buffalo, New York.*
Brigadier General Winfield Scott. *From the Conger Goodyear Manuscript Collection, Vol. 9. Courtesy of the Buffalo and Erie County Historical Society Research Library, Buffalo, New York.*
Brigadier General Eleazar Ripley. *From* Pictorial Field Book of the War of 1812.
Brigadier General Peter B. Porter. *From the Conger Goodyear Manuscript Collection, Vol. 9. Courtesy of the Buffalo and Erie County Historical Society Research Library, Buffalo, New York.*

Some of the personalities of the War of 1812–1815.

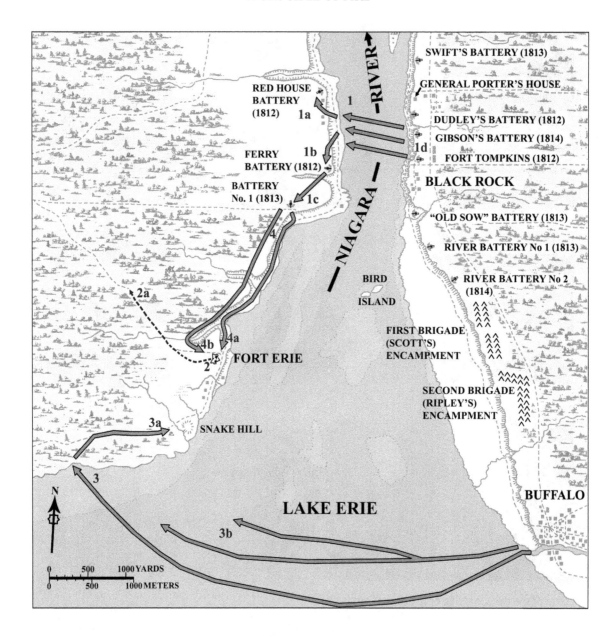

The American Invasion at Fort Erie, July 3, 1814

1. In the pre-dawn of July 3, 1814, the leading
    wave of General Scott's First Brigade (1) make
    their crossing of the Niagara River and land
    downriver from Fort Erie after encountering only
    minimal resistance from the riverside picket guard.
    Establishing a beachhead, American detachments
    quickly overrun the nearby British shore batteries
    at the Red House (1a), the ferry battery (1b), and
    battery No. 1 (1c). Additional waves of troops wait
    on the American shore for transport (1d).
2. At Fort Erie, the garrison is alerted and prepares
    their defences (2) while sending dispatch riders (2a)
    with news of the American invasion to General Riall.
3. Due to delays in the transport of troops across
    the greater distance and open water of Lake Erie,
    the initial wave of Ripley's pincer movement (3)
    is substantially delayed in reaching the Canadian
    shore and fails to arrive at Fort Erie as planned
    (3a), while subsequent waves encounter additional
    difficulties and delays (3b).
4. Without Ripley's support, Scott's force advances
    (4) on Fort Erie and establishes a partial encircle-
    ment (4a, 4b). Believing the situation makes it
    impossible to maintain any effective defence,
    Major Buck surrenders the position.

*   *June 7:* General Brown returns to Buffalo and
    assumes command of the Left Division, much
    to the displeasure of Brigadier General Scott,
    who presumed he would command the inva-
    sion force.
*   *July 2:* General Brown orders the invasion to
    commence the following night, following a set

of plans developed by him. The Second Brigade commander, Brigadier General Eleazar
Ripley, has doubts about the plan and presses
for changes. When these are not forthcoming, he officially submits his resignation on
the eve of the invasion. While Brown refuses
to accept the brigadier general's resignation
(feeling it is not in the best interests of the
nation) and publically ignores the implied
criticism of his leadership, the act leaves him
bitter and resentful, prejudicing his judgment
of any advice or recommendations subsequently submitted by Ripley.

*   *July 3:* American forces make an unopposed
    night crossing of the Niagara River, landing
    slightly downriver from the isolated and par-
    tially derelict fortification of Fort Erie. After
    forcing the small garrison of 137 British troops
    and Canadian militiamen to surrender,[2] the
    Americans secure their bridgehead and pre-
    pare to advance north, following the line of the
    Niagara River from its source at Fort Erie to its
    mouth at Newark (now Niagara-on-the-Lake).

General Brown's plan is to force a passage
to the other end of the river in order to arrive at
the shore of Lake Ontario by July 10. This is the
date when General Brown confidently believes
he will see Commodore Isaac Chauncey's fleet
arriving from the main American naval base

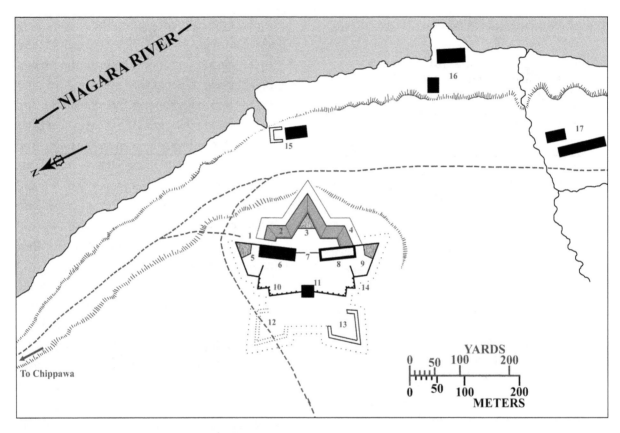

at Sackets Harbor, laden with reinforcements, ammunition, heavy artillery, and supplies.

- *July 4:* The First Brigade (Brigadier General Winfield Scott) marches north to the first of a series of rain-swollen creeks that feed into the Niagara River, only to find the northern bank is held by a substantially smaller but determined British force under Lieutenant Colonel Thomas Pearson. This British force successfully fulfils their order to delay the Americans by contesting each and every creek from Fort Erie to the Chippawa River, a distance of sixteen miles (twenty-six kilometers). By the end of that day, the British forces are secure in their main defensive line on the north bank of the Chippawa (Welland) River, facing Scott's frustrated troops

FORT ERIE, AS IT APPEARED AT THE TIME OF ITS SURRENDER ON JULY 3, 1814

1. Main entrance to the fort and outer gate
2. Eastern ravelin earthworks
3. Eastern ravelin artillery platform (designated for a 9-pounder gun)
4. Eastern ravelin ditch
5. Northeast demi-bastion with artillery platform (designated for a 12-pounder gun)
6. Northeast two-storey stone mess house and barracks (partially repaired and roofed in)
7. Inner gate
8. Southeast two-storey mess house and barracks (burned-out shell and unroofed)
9. Southeast demi-bastion with artillery platform (designated for a 12-pounder gun)
10. Western wooden picket wall
11. Western wall wooden blockhouse
12. Northwestern bastion foundation trace from pre-war period (no development construction work begun by this time)
13. Southwestern bastion foundation from the pre-war period (only consisting of a partial stone foundation rising to ground level)
14. Pre-war partially excavated and trace line of proposed ditch
15. Derelict lime-kiln foundation and small warehouse building
16. and 17. Civilian and military warehouses

on the south. With the only bridge connecting the two banks dismantled by the retreating British, and with insufficient daylight left to initiate any concrete action, the First Brigade withdraws a distance of about two miles (3.2 kilometers) and establishes their main encampment on the south side of Street's Creek.

- *July 5:* By dawn, the American position is reinforced by the arrival of the Second Brigade (Brigadier General Eleazar W. Ripley). The British are also reinforced by detachments of regular and militia infantry, artillery, and cavalry. However, during the course of the morning, detachments of British Native allies, sent only to maintain surveillance of the American positions, precipitate an escalating series of confrontations with American pickets. In response, General Brown decides to clear the forest west of his encampment of the British Native threat.

By noon, the American Third Brigade (Brigadier General Peter B. Porter) has also arrived, and is ordered to send a force of militia and American Native allies, supported by a detachment of regular troops, into the forest in order to clear the American flank. At the same time, within the British lines, Major General Phineas Riall has been drawn (by faulty reconnaissance that leads him to believe he has a temporary advantage of numbers, as well as his own personal biases about the ability and quality of the troops facing him) into making a series of mistaken conclusions about his enemy's current strength, quality, and

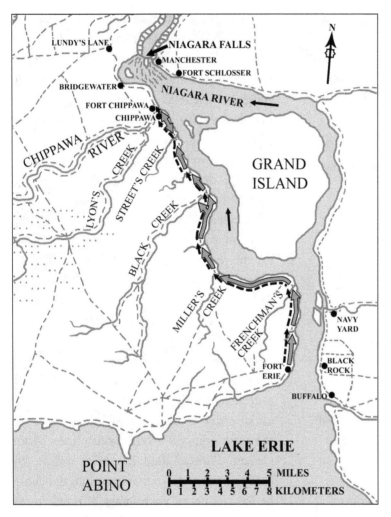

The riverbank route taken by the retreating British and advancing American forces on July 4, 1814.

dispositions. This leads him to make a fateful and ultimately disastrous decision to leave the security of his positions and go on the offensive to attack what he believes is only a part of a semi-trained enemy army, divided in location and unprepared to receive an attack.

Unfortunately for Riall, the army he faced was neither divided nor just semi-trained. As a result, in the ensuing Battle of Chippawa (for details see *The Tide of War*), the British make their attack with both a numerical and tactical disadvantage. As the conflict progresses and casualties mount, the British attack is ground to a halt by the intense American firepower coming from its strong static defensive line. Eventually, as additional American forces enter the battlefield, the savaged British force cedes the ground and retreats back to its defensive lines at the Chippawa River.

AMERICAN INVASION FORCE, JUNE 30, 1814[1]

Left Division (Major General Brown)
First Brigade (Brigadier General Winfield Scott)
Ninth Regiment (Major Leavenworth): 16 Officers, 332 Other Ranks* Total: 642 All Ranks
Eleventh Regiment (Colonel Campbell): 17 Officers, 416 Other Ranks* Total: 577 All Ranks
Twenty-Second Regiment (Colonel Brady [absent]): 12 Officers, 217 Other Ranks* Total: 287 All Ranks
Twenty-Fifth Regiment (Major Jesup): 16 Officers, 354 Other Ranks* Total: 619 All Ranks

Est. Total: 2,129 All Ranks

Second Brigade (Brigadier General Ripley)
Twenty-First Regiment (Lieutenant Colonel Miller): 25 Officers, 651 Other Ranks* Total: 917 All Ranks
Twenty-Third Regiment (Major McFarland): 8 Officers, 341 Other Ranks* Total: 496 All Ranks

Est. Total: 1,415 All Ranks

Third Brigade (Brigadier General Porter)
Fifth Pennsylvania Militia Regiment (Major Wood): 400–500 Other Ranks
New York Militia Regiments (Detachments)
Canadian Volunteers Regiment (Major Willcocks) (Detachment)

Est. Total: 830 All Ranks

Artillery (Major Hindman)
Captain Towson's Battery: 101 All Ranks
Captain Biddle's Battery: 104 All Ranks
Captain Richie's Battery: 138 All Ranks
Captain William's Battery: 73 All Ranks

Est. Total: 416 All Ranks

Cavalry (Captain Harris)
Est. Total: 1 Troop, 70–80 All Ranks

Native Allies (Lieutenant Colonel Granger)
Est. Total: 350–400 Warriors

N.B. For the * references above, see the Notes for additional details on the assessment of this force.

BRITISH TROOPS SURRENDERED AT FORT ERIE, JULY 3, 1814[2]

8th (King's) Regiment: 1 Officer (Major)
Royal Artillery: 1 Officer (Lieutenant), 21 Gunners
100th Regiment: 4 Officers (1 Captain, 2 Lieutenants, 1 Ensign), 4 Sergeants, 3 Musicians, 101 Rank and File

CHAPTER 2

Manoeuvring for Advantage: The Niagara Frontier, July 6–23, 1814

In the aftermath of the stunning defeat of the British forces at the Battle of Chippawa, the impact upon the respective forces involved was dramatic. On the British side, Major General Phineas Riall had to privately come to terms with the fact that he had made a serious strategic error by leaving his strong defensive position on the Chippawa River to attack the Americans in the open. However, publically he could not afford to admit to this failure, and in his post-battle report Riall simply referred to his attack as "not attended with the success that I had hoped for."[1] While he reluctantly acknowledged the Americans had improved their quality of battlefield discipline, he also chose to claim that the Americans had fielded an overwhelming number of troops in their line of battle, estimating the American force at over 6,000 versus his own 1,800.

While convenient, this reasoning also ignored the contradictions that arose from his pre-battle justification for attacking the Americans in the first place instead of remaining securely on the defensive behind his lines at Chippawa: First, that he had believed he was fighting only a part of a divided enemy army, with the majority still involved in investing Fort Erie, which, in fact, had already surrendered. Second, that he did not anticipate that once the battle began his troops would be standing face-to-face with the enemy for an extended period of time and exchanging volleys at point-blank range. In other words, if the Americans really had openly fielded that many troops in the first place, neither Riall nor any other competent commander would have been so foolish as to attack them on their own ground. Likewise, had these "superior numbers"[2]

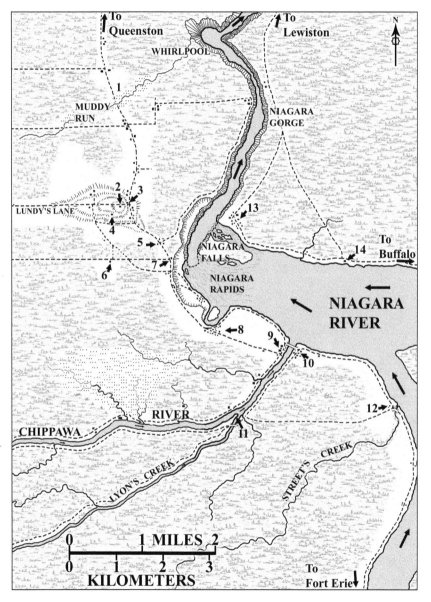

LOCATIONS AROUND THE GREAT FALLS OF NIAGARA, JULY 1814

1. Cook's bog, or "Muddy Run"
2. The Lundy's Lane church on the hilltop
3. Johnson's Tavern at the Lundy's Lane/Portage Road crossroad
4. Buchner farmstead
5. Forsyth's Tavern
6. Haggai Skinner's farmstead
7. Mrs. Wilson's tavern
8. Bridgewater Mills
9. British fortifications at the Chippawa River
10. Chippawa Village
11. Weishoun's Point
12. Ussher's farmstead
13. Village of Manchester (Niagara Falls, New York)
14. Fort Schlosser

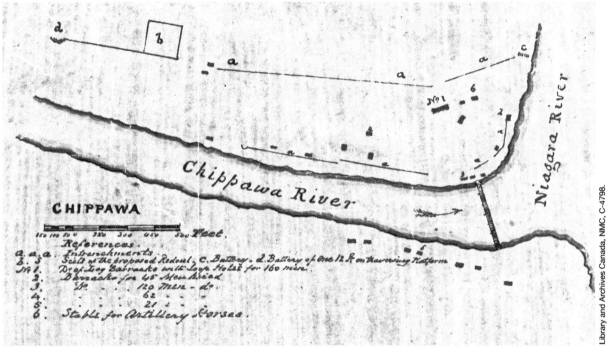

A pre-war map of the defences and bridge at the strategic junction of the Chippawa (Welland) and Niagara Rivers. Inset from a larger map of the Niagara frontier.

appeared during the initial or even central course of the engagement, he would have gone on the defensive or broken off much earlier, recognizing that he had absolutely no reserve to counterbalance the American advantage of numbers.

Fortunately for Riall, both of his superior commanders (Lieutenant General Gordon Drummond and Sir George Prevost) chose to overlook this contradiction, as both recognized the calamitous effect this defeat of British regulars by an equivalent number of American troops could have on morale and the further prosecution of the war effort. Consequently, they both chose to publicly support Riall's line of reasoning of bravely fighting against overwhelming American numbers and being forced by weight of numbers alone to withdraw, in good order, to their original defensive positions. On the other hand, privately, both senior commanders saw that this European-style collision of lines had produced the unexpected result of proving that the Americans were now fully capable of fielding an army that was able to contend with whatever the British had to offer; and the humiliating defeats and debacles of the American army over the previous two years were now things of the past.

In response, both Riall and Drummond resolved to take the American army on the Niagara far more seriously. In a similar manner, Drummond decided that he might need to take a more immediate and direct command of his troops if the military situation continued to deteriorate.

This battlefield defeat and the casualty losses also had a significant impact on Riall's auxiliary troops (the part-time embodied militia regiments and Native allies). Virtually all of the surviving British Native allied warriors saw the defeat as a threatening omen and quit the Chippawa position, leaving only a determined handful of warriors under the leadership of the Native war chief, John Norton. Similarly, many of the locally-raised militiamen, who had little previous experience of a conflict this intense, went AWOL (absent without leave), either because they had seen their fill of combat or had decided that in light of the American victory and the prospect of their further advance into Upper Canada, the threat posed by the invaders to their families, homes, and properties was a higher

Chippawa. E. Walsh, artist, 1804. A pre-war image looking west up the Chippawa (Welland) River from the position of the original bridge. The small hamlet of Chippawa is on the left (south) and British defensive installations on the right (north) bank of the river.

A view of the Chippawa (Welland) River, looking west from Chippawa toward Weishoun's Point, 2013.

(Above) *Chippawa Village*. Sempronius Stretton, artist, 1804. The view looking south across the Chippawa River bridge toward the small village of Chippawa in 1804. Neither the bridge nor the buildings survived the war intact. (Below) The same view today (2013).

personal priority than remaining with the defeated army. In both cases, this defection deprived Riall of most of his light troops and weakened his position.

Desperate to replace these losses, orders were immediately dispatched to Burlington Heights (Hamilton), Long Point, and York (Toronto) for all remaining regular detachments and militia to consolidate their forces on the Niagara, despite having to, in the process, leave their former garrison positions virtually undefended.

On the other side of the field, although having gained a significant victory, Major General Jacob Brown recognized that this success had only been achieved at the cost of a substantial number of casualties, especially from the First Brigade, a force that had trained intensively that spring. Nor were any similarly trained recruits immediately available to take their place. In addition, having successfully regained the far (north) bank of the Chippawa, the British continued to block the only road available to reach the mouth of the Niagara River and Brown's expected rendezvous of his victorious army with Chauncey's fleet on July 10. After detailing his troops to evacuate the wounded and prisoners across the Niagara River and bury the dead of both sides in long common graves upon the field of battle during the course of July 7, General Brown opted against making a direct assault upon the British Chippawa defences. Instead, on July

8, the depleted First Brigade (Brigadier Winfield Scott) was ordered to provide a diversionary show of force at the mouth of the Chippawa River, opposite the main British positions, while the Second Brigade (Brigadier General Eleazar W. Ripley) and Third Brigade (Brigadier Peter B. Porter) were to make a surprise outflanking march to the west and then force a crossing of the Chippawa River at Weishoun's Point, located at the junction of Lyon's Creek and the Chippawa River, some two miles (3.2 kilometers) upriver.

However, despite the extensive amount of construction work done over the previous two days to prepare this route, the trail remained impassable to the heavy wagons and artillery accompanying this column, while the additional delays and noise made in forcing a wider trail through the dense forest allowed the British to detect the movement and mount a defence that stalled the American crossing.

Although the American advance was temporarily halted, General Riall received faulty reports that the Americans had succeeded in making their landing on the north bank and were threatening to cut off his line of retreat toward Queenston. As a result, Riall decided to abandon his main defence line and withdraw his army toward Queenston Heights.

As the leading elements of troops began their retreat north, they came upon the Volunteer Battalion of Incorporated Militia, marching south in the

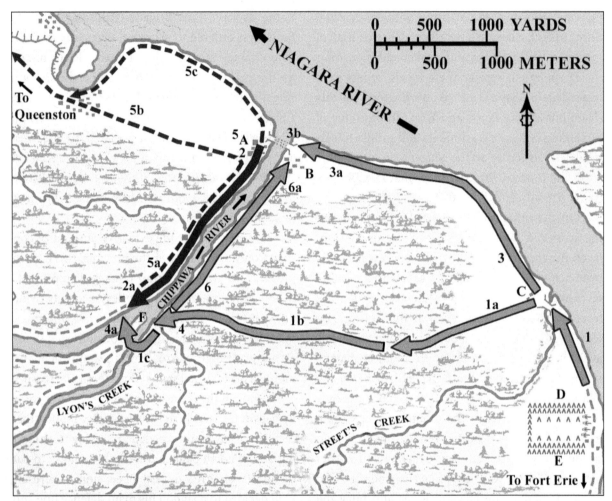

THE AMERICAN FLANKING MOVEMENT AND ENGAGEMENT AT WEISHOUN'S POINT, JULY 8, 1814

A. Chippawa fortifications and main British lines
B. Chippawa Village
C. Ussher's farmstead
D. Brigadier General Scott's (First Brigade) encampment
E. Brigadier General Ripley's (Second Brigade) encampment
F. Weishoun's Point

(*N.B.* 1, 2, and 3 occur simultaneously.)

1. Attempting a flanking movement around the British positions, the American army moves out from its encampment (D, E) on July 8 (1). Brigadier General Ripley's (Second Brigade) and Brigadier General Porter's (Third Brigade) move west (1a) to follow a narrow trackway leading to Weishoun's Point (C-F), only to find that despite previous work to widen the trail, it is still impassable for the column's heavy wagons and artillery. Additional work to clear and widen the roadway slows the advance (1b) and creates significant noise, effectively ruining any chance of surprise. Reaching the bank of Lyon's Creek (1c) at Weishoun's Point (F), they find British units already in situ on the other side of the Chippawa (Welland) River (2a).
2. Receiving reports of activity on the American side of the Chippawa River behind Weishoun's Point (F), Major General Riall sends detachments of infantry and artillery under Lieutenant Colonel Pearson to occupy the position opposite the point (2-2a).
3. Brigadier General Scott's (First Brigade) (3) marches along the riverbank road (3a) with orders to make a strong diversionary show of force at the Chippawa village (B) to persuade the British that an attempt would be made to cross there.
4. Faced with the loss of surprise and British forces in opposition, Brigadier General Ripley halts the advance and sends word to Major General Brown. Brown arrives (4) and takes command. He then orders that the attack recommence and begins construction of a pontoon bridge while under fire (4a).
5. Faced with Scott's apparent plan to cross at the bridge, Major General Riall (5) is unable to send reinforcements to Pearson (2a). Receiving erroneous reports the Americans had succeeded in crossing at Weishoun's Point, Riall believes his position has been turned and orders a general evacuation from the Chippawa line (A) (5a, 5b, 5c).
6. Receiving reports from Scott (3b) that the British are evacuating their defences at Chippawa (A), Brown discontinues his bridge-building and marches the Second and Third Brigades (6) along the Chippawa riverbank toward the bridge (6a) to unite his force before making his crossing at the now burned-out village of Chippawa (B).

A modern (2013) view of the location where Ripley's force attempted to construct a pontoon bridge to cross the Chippawa (Welland) River

1. Lyon's Creek
2. Weishoun's Point
3. Chippawa (Welland) River
4. The north bank, where the British established their positions
5. To Chippawa and the Niagara River
6. The rotted wooden pilings of a bridge similar in construction to that built across the Chippawa at the time of the war

direction of the Chippawa River. This regiment had been rapidly pushed over from York in response to Riall's call for reinforcements and had just made a forced march to join the line. According to one officer of that regiment, marching a distance of nine miles (14.5 kilometers) under a hot and sweltering sky that increasingly threatened a repetition of the previous day's thunderstorms, the men were "expecting to see the enemy every moment."[3]

They had just reached the crossroads at Lundy's Lane, some two miles (3.2 kilometers) short of the Chippawa, and halted for a short break, when supply wagons and limbered artillery appeared on the road ahead, followed immediately by columns of red-coated infantry, "accompanied by hundreds of women and children, besides men on foot and in vehicles,"[4] all pressing north with some speed. Riders from the column now brought new orders from General Riall for the Incorporated Militia to move off the road and take up a defensive position on the hillside. Once the column had passed through, if the Americans had not appeared or attacked, the regiment was then to act as the rearguard for the duration of the march back to Queenston.

Remaining as ordered, the Incorporated Militia began their trek back the way they had just come. Only this time they had to maintain a steady watch to their rear and flanks for any appearance by the pursuing enemy. Finally, under a torrent of rain, the Incorporated Militia reached Queenston around 10:00 p.m., having marched a total of nearly eighteen miles (twenty-nine kilometers) that day. They were also hungry, for they had not had the opportunity to prepare food since early that morning:

> [At Queenston] a short halt was made ... where we got a drink of muddy sulphur water [from a stream] that crossed the road, and had served to each man and officer about half a pound of bread that had been brought in an open wagon, and was pretty well filled with dust and gravel, gladly eating and drinking as could be got ...[5]

However, the army was not destined to get any further reprieve, for after only a brief rest period, orders were received to move on toward Newark (Niagara-on-the-Lake) and Fort George. This order came as something of a surprise to most of the troops. The general expectation being that some defensive action would take place on the old battlefield of Queenston because the position had been substantially strengthened since October 1812 and now consisted of good defensive artillery emplacements, blockhouses, and barracks, as well as relatively secure flanks provided by the river gorge on one side and the escarpment on the other. Instead:

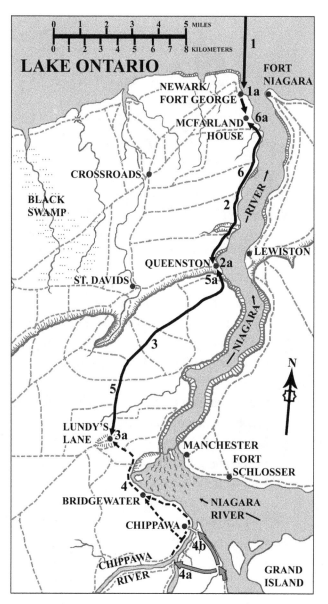

THE ROUTE TAKEN BY THE INCORPORATED MILITIA REGIMENT TO REACH CHIPPAWA, AND THEIR RETURN AS PART OF THE BRITISH ARMY'S RETREAT, JULY 6–8, 1814

1. The Incorporated Militia Regiment arrives in ships from York (1) and disembarks at Fort George (1a) at sunset on July 6.
2. The regiment marches to Queenston (2) and encamps for the night, 10:00 p.m. (2a).
3. At dawn on July 8, the regiment is ordered to march up along the Portage Road (3) to Chippawa. It reaches the Lundy's Lane cross-roads (3a) where it halts at around 2:00 p.m.
4. The British forces retreat from the Chippawa River (4) in the face of the American attacks at Weishoun's Point (4a) and the Chippawa Bridge (4b).
5. After seeing the British forces pass, the Incorporated Militia retires as the rearguard of the column (5) to the Queenston Heights (5a), where it halts around 10:00 p.m.
6. Upon the British column retreating to Newark (6), the Incorporated Militia again acts as rear-guard until it reaches the McFarland house (6a), where it halts and encamps at around midnight.

During the halt at Queenston the guns were dismantled and … the stores hauled out of a small fort built on the side of the mountain…. It had but lately been finished, and appeared sufficient to stand a siege. After the guns and stores had been removed, the block house was set on fire and destroyed, so that it could not be used by the enemy …[6]

The historic site of McFarland House, 2013. It is now a museum operated by the Niagara Parks Commission.

Despite the reference that the stores were removed, large stockpiles actually remained inside the buildings and were destroyed, including virtually the entire British stock of spades and pickaxes, as well as other entrenching and construction tools — a loss that was to have significant and severe repercussions upon the ability of the British army to wage its siege campaign at Fort Erie in the ensuing months. (For details see the forthcoming *The Ashes of War*.)

Continuing north, Riall moved his troops on with some rapidity, concerned that the Americans might still outflank him or cut him off. After a hurried march, he reached Fort George in the early hours of July 9 and immediately set about developing plans for a new line of defence, while the men of the Incorporated Militia once again provided the rearguard, as later recorded by Lieutenant Henry Ruttan:

Were halted at McFarland's, a large deserted brick house about a mile outside the fort as a piquet guard, until morning, the remainder of our force passing on to the fort. After placing sentries, all found a resting place on the floor of the house and ground of the orchard nearby, until daylight, from whence we could see the tents of the enemy, established on the mountain, six miles from us.

After daylight we were marched [to Fort Mississauga] … and encamped within range of the fort, remaining there several days …[7]

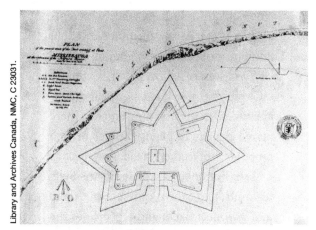

An 1814 plan of Fort Mississauga, constructed on the western bank of the Niagara River where it flows into Lake Ontario.

Captain Archibald McLean, also of that regiment, later recorded his impression of this march in a letter to his father:

> We arrived here [Fort Mississauga] about ten o'clock, having marched about eight and twenty miles dur'g the [previous] day, which was one of the warmest we have seen here this summer, and what added to the fatigues was the immense clouds of dust in which we were constantly kept by the Dragoons and Artillery ...[8]

Back at the Chippawa River, General Brown ferried the First and Second Brigades over the river

The gateway to Fort Mississauga, 2013. Maintained by Parks Canada, Fort Mississauga is located within the fairways of the Niagara-on-the-Lake golf course, which was itself land formerly assigned for Crown use.

Inside the earthworks of Fort Mississauga, 2013. The central blockhouse is reputedly partially built of bricks scavenged from the burnt-out shells of nearby homes, after they were torched by the retreating Americans in December 1813.

during the night of July 8/9, while ordering a dis-gruntled General Porter's Third Brigade to repair the bridge and then bring forward the main bag-gage train. At this juncture, several units of the Pennsylvania militias decided that their service in the battle at Chippawa had fulfilled any further mil-itary obligations on their part. Standing upon their state's legal military rights and statutory limitations not to serve beyond their national boundaries, they ignored their previous agreement to serve in the invasion and refused to advance farther, forcing Brown to capitulate to their demands and detach them from the army with orders to return to Fort Erie and assist in the occupation of that position. Pressing forward during the afternoon of the ninth, Brown's troops met with only token resist-ance from British picket detachments and reached the "Heights" at Queenston. From this vantage point the general could see across the plain to Lake Ontario and his expected place of rendezvous with Commodore Chauncey. Here the American army encamped and was subsequently joined by Porter's brigade and additional reinforcements. As one American officer wrote,

How shall I describe the emotions with which we drank in our first view from Queenston Heights.... Beneath our feet were a small village and a broad expanse of open plain ... literally white with tents. Long lines of troops were under arms; col-umns in motion; guards coming in and out; Divisions of artillery at drill; videttes of Cavalry at speed; and Aides and Staff-officers ... in earnest movement. There was no display of gaudy plumes or rich trappings; but in their stead, grey-jackets — close-buttoned — plain white belts, steel hilts, and brown muskets; but there were bayonets fixed, and a glance of the eye would show that those boxes were filled with ball-cartridges.... This, then, was no mere parade — no stage play, for effect — it was simple and sublime reality — IT WAS WAR.... It would be difficult

LOCATIONS ALONG THE LOWER (NORTHERN) REACHES OF THE NIAGARA RIVER AS IT FLOWS OUT FROM THE GORGE AT QUEENSTON TO LAKE ONTARIO

A. Fort Mississauga
B. Newark (Niagara-on-the-Lake)
C. Fort George
D. McFarland house
E. Fort Niagara
F. Youngstown
G. Lewiston
H. Queenston
I. "Heights" of Queenston (American encampment)
J. St. Davids
K. Crossroads (Virgil)

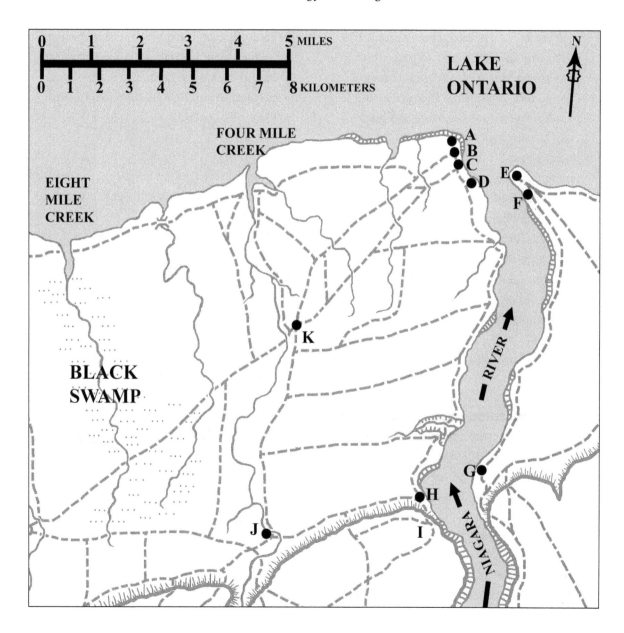

to transfer … an adequate impression of the military sights and sounds which give animation to the scene. The various guards mounting; the drills and parades; the regimental beats and bugle-calls, converging from so many points at once; retreat beating and parade at sundown; tattoo, at nine o'clock; and above all, the fine old spirit-stirring reveille of Baron Steuben, at the earliest dawn of the day. These beats commenced, generally with the regiment on the extreme right; then the next; the next; and so on; till the whole circumference was one grand chorus of the most thrilling martial music …

— Lieutenant David B. Douglass[9]

Seeing no point in attacking Riall at his well-defended enclave at the mouth of the river until Chauncey arrived with reinforcements and a proper siege train of artillery, General Brown took the opportunity to restore the daily regimen of drills and training for his troops.

First Brigade Order, July 11, 1814

Everything is to be done this forenoon to put the Brigade in fighting order. The arms and accoutrements are to be carefully examined — Clothing washed — the men shaved and where necessary the hair cropped. There will be an inspection and drill this evening to commence at 4 o'clock …

— W. Scott, B. Genl.[10]

This action was not only to bring the new units and reinforcements up to standard, but also to re-establish a degree of discipline, for in addition to the defections by elements of the Pennsylvania militia, there were complaints from Canadian civilians now living under American occupation of looting and other depredations taking place — particularly by elements of Porter's brigade, including the detested "Canadian Volunteers" Regiment, a corps principally composed of former Canadian settlers who had turned renegade and opted to fight on the side of the Americans. While their orders were

(Facing, above) *Queenston Heights*. F. Hall, artist, 1816. The spectacular panoramic view from the top of the Niagara escarpment above Queenston. (Facing, below) The same perspective today (2013).

1. Queenston
2. Vrooman's Point
3. Lewiston, New York
4. Fort George/Newark
5. Fort Niagara
6. The north shore of Lake Ontario/York (Toronto)

View from Queenston Heights. G.Heriot, artist, circa 1805. A view of the village of Queenston and the Niagara River as seen from Portage Road as it ascends the escarpment.

Queenston. Looking upriver (south) toward the Heights above Queenston, where the Americans made their encampment as they waited in vain for Chauncey to arrive with his fleet.

officially only to elicit information on the British dispositions and intentions, these renegades had previously engaged in repeated examples of using their military positions as a cover for exacting personal vendettas and engaging in pillaging, making arrests without cause or warrant, and wantonly burning Loyalist homes and crops — and were therefore not likely to be restrained in this instance. As a result, within days of the appearance of the "Canadian Volunteers" in the surrounding communities, the Americans saw an escalation in reports of retaliations, with sentries being attacked and patrols being fired on, to the point where no individual was able to leave the encampment without fear of disappearing without a trace.

Internally too, circumstances deteriorated when the previously dormant irritations and simmering personality conflicts between the various commanders and their respective subordinate officers erupted to the surface once General Brown's official report on the Battle of Chippawa was issued. This report praised Winfield Scott but omitted mention of several of his junior commanders, leading to hard feelings on their part and jealousy by the officers in the other brigades. Over the next two weeks, a war of letters erupted between members of the officer corps, undermining the unity and authority of the army's leadership. This was exacerbated by the fact that several of the letters were printed

The "Heights" at Queenston and the southern end of the Niagara River Gorge, 2013.

in the *Buffalo Gazette* and other newspapers for all to see. So strong were the resultant feelings that Major Jesup, commander of the Twenty-Fifth Regiment, subsequently announced his desire to leave the army:

> I am anxious myself to leave the army — the cursed publications in the Buffaloe Gazette and other papers, relative to the action of the 5th have completely disgusted me ... there is scarcely a word of truth in any of these publications.... The Gen'l Order published after the action ... has found its way into the paper, is an insult to all who were engaged on that day ...
> — Major Jesup to Major Trimble,
> July 23, 1814[11]

In turn, Winfield Scott responded to the criticism coming from his own juniors by officially submitting his own resignation. Anxious to heal the schism, Brown refused to accept Scott's resignation and quickly issued a second report, including details and commendations for services rendered by the affronted officers (almost to the point of absurdity) that persuaded these gentlemen to reconsider their positions.

During this same period, General Riall had been steadily improving his defensive positions at the mouth of the Niagara River[*12] (see chart on page 60) and looked hopefully for the sight of Yeo's fleet arriving from Kingston with reinforcements, food, and ammunition. But in this he was to be as disappointed as his American counterpart. Expecting Brown to press forward and use his larger force to invest the forts, Riall correctly interpreted the reason for Brown's delay and was forced to consider the prospect that if Chauncey did arrive soon, the combined force would encircle the British position and could well force its surrender or destruction under the numerous guns on board the American fleet. After making a study of the capabilities of his fortifications to defend against such an onslaught, and concluding that they were insufficient to ensure a successful defence, Riall decided to pre-emptively withdraw most of his forces back toward Burlington, while leaving holding garrisons in the three forts, thus hopefully placing the American commander in the position of facing the prospect of making simultaneous attacks in two directions, or suffering an attack on his rear should he decide to move on either the forts or the main British force.

> Sir, The enemy still occupy the same position ... and are I imagine waiting for the arrival of their fleet to furnish them with heavy ordnance for their operations against our forts.... The fall of these places is inevitable if vigorously attacked, unless the besiegers are interrupted in their operations or a diversion made to draw their attention elsewhere.... Having left in Forts George, Missassauga and Niagara such garrisons as the officers of engineers shall consider necessary for their actual defence, I shall move ... towards Burlington with between 8 and 900 men. I have directed Colonel Scott to meet me at the 40 with the 103rd, the militia collected at Burlington ... and the whole of the Indians that can be assembled and with this force get into the enemy's rear by the Short Hills and Lundy's Lane. I have also directed Lieut-Colonel Battersby to move from York with the Glengarry Light Infantry, as I conceive the protection of that place at this moment a secondary consideration and that it is not likely to be attacked as the enemy's whole attention seems to be engaged with the attack of our forts. If ... you are forwarding reinforcements to this quarter, part of them may be left at York ... but I am decidedly of opinion that every means should be taken to

create such a force as will make the discomfiture and annihilation of the enemy beyond a doubt ...

— General Riall to General Drummond July 12, 1814[13]

In addition to the above official command report, personal letters, such as one from Captain Archibald McLean of the Incorporated Militia, painted a fairly confident picture of the British prospects at this time:

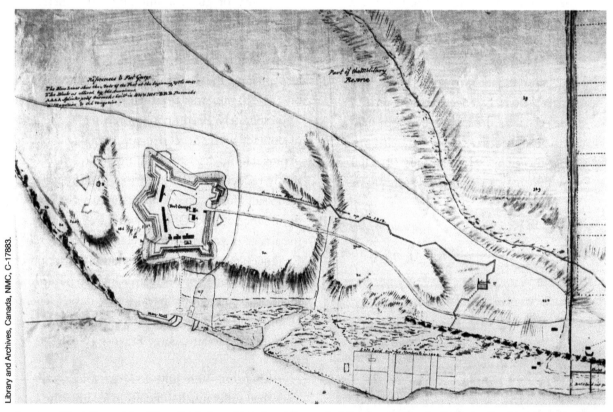

A map of Fort George and its adjacent earthworks at the end of the war. Built principally by the Americans in the summer of 1813, these positions were then retaken by the British in December 1813. The outline of the original pre-war British fortifications, which were destroyed in the Battle of Fort George (May 27, 1813), can be traced below and to the south (left) of the rebuilt fort.

13 July ... Since we came to this place [Fort Mississauga], two hundred of our men under Col. Robinson have been out about half way to Queenston for forage, but did not meet any of the enemy, tho' they are now in possession of that place in numbers uncertain. Last night a force ... advanced in order to cut off our piquets if possible, but they found them too alert and after exchanging some shots they retired. There has been no loss on our side except a Corp'l & three or four men of the King's [8th (King's) Regiment] missing, the enemy's loss is uncertain, but that they have lost a General seems to be undoubted.... We have frequent alarms here but do not expect to have anything to do till the enemy's fleet comes up — We are pretty well prepared for an attack, hav'g three months provisions in store, plenty of guns, ammunition and men, and I hope plenty of courage ...[14]

As confident and optimistic as this last letter appears, the reality for the British position on the Niagara was drastically different. As well as desperately needing reinforcements, the loss of contact with the entire southern flank of the peninsula and its vital farming centres had drastically reduced the availability of fresh supplies to feed Riall's forces. In addition, the American naval dominance of Lake Ontario and the expectation of the arrival of an American fleet under Commodore Chauncey made any waterborne transportation of additional food supplies from Kingston hazardous in the extreme. Over the next few days, General Drummond recorded the extent of his difficulties in his reports to Sir George Prevost:

Kingston, 10th July, 1814 ... I fear we shall suffer much difficulty in feeding [the army on the Niagara] ... Mr. Couche having received a letter from Mr. Turquand this day, expressing his apprehension of

The present-day (2013) reconstruction of one of the large wooden barracks at the national historic site of Fort George.

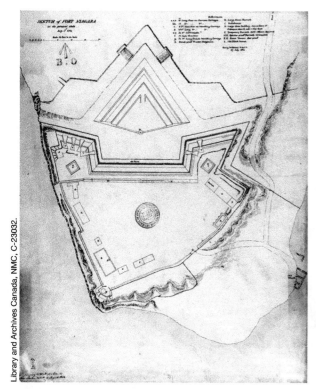

Fort Niagara in 1814.

Kingston, 13th July, 1814 … Major General Riall calls upon me strongly for, and indeed expects, reinforcements, but Your Excellency must be aware that I have not a man to send him and that those expected from the Lower Province cannot be calculated at arriving higher than Cornwall before the latter end of the week … as the troops cannot be forwarded without provisions, I have requested Sir James Yeo to send his two brigs immediately, with as much flour and pork as they can carry, to York and Burlington.[16]

Kingston, 15th July 1814 … I have received letters from Colonel Scott at Burlington stating his intention of moving to the Forty Mile Creek, his force at present being the 103rd Regiment, a detachment of the 19th Dragoons, about 1000 militia and some Indians…. I have disapproved of this movement and directed him to return and retain his post at Burlington, as well as to dismiss all the too young, elderly, and inactive men of the militia … and to keep only those of healthy and serviceable appearance … as that it would be impossible to provision such numbers…. Although I should

a failure in the article of flour, which is totally impossible to assist them in from Kingston, from the want of means of transport from hence. I have even been under the necessity of taking twelve batteaux from the [boat transport] brigades which arrived yesterday [from Montreal] to forward the 89th regiment to York …[15]

have wished it, I am apprehensive that I shall not have it in my power to forward any further re-inforcements to the Right Division from the inability of the Commissariat to supply provisions, and in fact dread their failing in due supplies to those already ordered there ...[17]

Rations had already been cut the previous month and nonessential personnel and dependents had been ordered to be evacuated to Lower Canada to reduce the number of mouths requiring supplies, but it was still not enough. Consequently, on July 13, the following drastic measures were enacted:

General Order ... All women and children following the army above Kingston are to be immediately put upon half their usual rations until further orders and it is recommended as many as possible should be sent down to Kingston by every opportunity ...[18]

(Facing, above) *Fort Niagara*. H. Slade, artist. This post-war view of Fort Niagara shows the garrison as it appeared during the war, with the roofs of the "French Castle" and blockhouses removed to facilitate the mounting of artillery. The main (riverside) gate of the fort from 1812–15 can be clearly seen, as can the (by then collapsing) perimeter picket walls. (Facing, below) The same view in 2012.

Kingston, 16 July 1814 ... So much alarmed am I, even with the present numbers, that I have directed all the women and children of the [regular] troops to be sent down from Niagara, Burlington and York, and the families of the militia and Indians to be placed on half allowance ...[19]

Because even at full quota a regimental wife was officially entitled to only a half ration and dependent children one-third of a man's, this additional cut reduced their subsistence to starvation levels and caused significant hardship for these dependents, especially in the case of those with the Incorporated Militia Regiment. (For details, see *Redcoated Ploughboys* by this author.)

Meanwhile, the contest for strategic advantage between the two armies continued in the form of numerous skirmishes between detachments and pickets. One such event (alluded to in the previous letter of July 13) took place on the night of July 12/13, when a detachment of three officers and thirty-four other ranks from the 8th (King's) Regiment, under the command of Major Thomas Evans, were sent on a reconnaissance mission from Fort George to the area just outside the village and on the road leading to the Crossroads (Virgil). This was going to be the route the British army was to follow the next morning in its partial withdrawal in the direction of

Burlington Heights and therefore required checking before the troops moved out. During the course of this mission, they came across evidence of an American presence nearby. Leaving a detachment of five men to watch this position, Major Evans and the remainder had moved on to complete their mission when a single shot was heard coming from the direction of the detached picket. When no further sounds ensued, the main body continued forward, only to suddenly be fired on — from the rear!

What had occurred was that the suspected American presence was, in fact, a sizeable force of around 120 Third Brigade militia, under Brigadier General Swift, who were on a similar reconnaissance mission. Detecting the smaller British detachment, the Americans were quickly able to overwhelm the men before advancing to attack the larger force. According to the British version, only a single shot was fired by the detachment, and this shot killed General Swift. According to the American version, this shot came from one of the British soldiers who had already surrendered and was being interrogated by the general. What is not explained is how a captured enemy soldier had been allowed to retain a loaded musket and ammunition in order to be able to shoot Swift.

In the ensuing firefight between the two principal forces, no advantage accrued to either side, and after a sharp exchange of shots, which resulted in a few men being wounded, both units withdrew to their respective lines.

The following morning, in accordance with General Riall's plan of withdrawal, the bulk of the British and Canadian force moved out for Twenty Mile Creek, where it was joined by the reinforcements of regulars and militia from Burlington Heights; with this augmented force, General Riall took the opportunity to reorganize his patchwork collection of regiments and detachments into four separate brigades.[20] (See chart on page 61.)

In the American camp, the reports of Riall's movement seemed to be contradicted by the evidence that the forts at the river mouth remained actively defended. Consequently, General Brown became more and more concerned about his plan of campaign, as the advantage he had gained by his victory at Chippawa seemed to be slipping away. The day of rendezvous with Chauncey was now well past and there were still no sign of sails on the horizon. In addition, his current supply lines were restricted to the land routes that ran from Buffalo to Queenston via Lewiston or Chippawa, the latter of which had suffered at least one attack and the capture of a supply train by raiding parties of Canadian militias and Native allies. Reaching the end of his patience on July 13, Brown dispatched a strongly worded letter to Chauncey, demanding to know what was happening:

My Dear Sir ... I arrived at this place on the 10th, as I assured you that by the blessing of God I would.... Meet me on the lakeshore, north of Fort George, with your fleet, and we will be able ... to settle a plan of operations that will break the power of the enemy in Upper Canada and that in the course of a short time; at all events, let me hear from you. I have looked for your fleet with the greatest anxiety since the **tenth**.... We can threaten Forts George and Niagara and carry Burlington Heights and York and proceed direct to Kingston and carry that place. For Gods sake let me see you.... If you conclude to meet me at the head of the lake, and that immediately, have the goodness to bring the guns and troops that I have ordered from the Harbour; at all events have the politeness to let me know what aid I am to expect from the fleet of Lake Ontario ...

— General Brown to Commodore
Chauncey, July 13, 1814[21]

He then issued an order for his senior officers to attend his headquarters the following day to consider their options for the continuation of the campaign. At this council of officers, General Brown outlined their current position, including the prospect of Chauncey not arriving for some days, the exposed vulnerability of the supply line from Buffalo, and the British redeployment from the forts at the mouth of the river. He then looked for his brigade commanders' advice.

General Ripley argued that any assault against the forts would be useless without the firepower of the guns and reinforcements that were to be brought up by the fleet. Instead, he proposed that his brigade immediately march in pursuit of Riall, to be closely followed by Scott's and Porter's troops, and that by marching through the night they could then make a dawn attack and defeat Riall's army before it could be reinforced, thus leaving the forts open for reduction at leisure. In this matter, Ripley was supported by General Porter. In reply, General Scott opposed this plan, arguing that any movement away from the river, without previously eliminating the garrisons at Fort George, Fort Mississauga, and Fort Niagara, would expose the American flanks and tenuous supply lines to the threat of attack from the British entrenched positions, as well as making a link-up with Chauncey more difficult once he arrived. As General Brown invariably tended to agree with General Scott, the predictable result was the decision to eliminate the forts before continuing with the campaign. Unfortunately, this choice was also

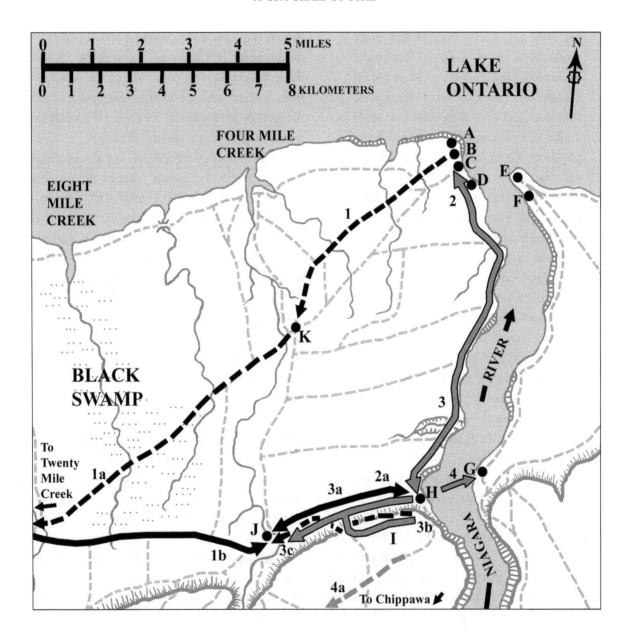

MOVE AND COUNTERMOVE, JULY 13–24, 1814

A. Fort Mississauga
B. Newark (Niagara-on-the-Lake)
C. Fort George
D. McFarland house
E. Fort Niagara
F. Youngstown
G. Lewiston
H. Queenston
I. "Heights" of Queenston (American encampment)
J. St. Davids
K. Crossroads (Virgil)

1. July 13. To prevent a threatened encirclement, General Riall makes a strategic withdrawal with the bulk of his force (1-1a) from their positions at the mouth of the Niagara River (ABC) toward the Twenty Mile Creek, leaving behind garrisons in each of the three forts. Subsequently, detachments of the British force advance (1b) and re-establish picket positions at St. Davids (J).
2. July 20. General Brown orders the abandonment of the American positions at Queenston (H, I) and advances (2) to within sight of Fort George (C). There he begins to construct siege entrenchments. With the departure of the Americans, British detachments at St. Davids (J) advance (2a) and occupy Queenston (H) and its dominant "Heights" (I), severing the American supply line from Fort Erie.
3. July 22. With news that Chauncey's fleet and reinforcements will not be coming, General Brown orders the abandonment of the attempt to besiege the British positions at the mouth of the Niagara River and retires his army (3) toward Queenston (H). Finding the position occupied by British advance units (2a), American advance units engage in skirmishes with their British counterparts, resulting in a fluctuating engagement that moves from Queenston (H) and the Heights (I) along and below the escarpment (3a, 3b, 3c) to St. Davids (J).
4. July 23. General Brown decides to secure and shorten his supply line from Fort Erie via Chippawa. He orders the removal of all superfluous baggage and supplies (4) across the Niagara River to Lewiston (G) before marching his troops south along the Portage Road (4a).

seen as confirming Brown's previously voiced poor opinion of Ripley's military capabilities, as well as revealing the lower status in which he held the judgment of his militia commander, Porter, resulting in further alienation of those two commanders' support for the campaign.

The following day (July 15), Brown ordered Porter's brigade to cut off communications between the garrisons and Riall's main force. After pushing in the British pickets at Fort Mississauga and coming under some fire from the fort's guns, Porter decided his duty was done and returned to his camp with the bulk of his force, having suffered only two casualties to the British fire. Behind him he left only a thin screen of pickets, which soon came under the predatory attentions of detachments of Riall's Canadian militias. The American supply lines weren't free from threat either, and the local populace had kept Riall well informed of the American movements and dispositions, allowing five men from a detachment of New York cavalry and another supply convoy to be captured the next day. These annoyances and losses quickly prompted a strong reaction from General Porter:

> I have to report the loss of five men of Capt. Boughton's fine company of New York Cavalry made prisoners. They are victims of your own generous policy of suffering the inhabitants who profess neutrality to remain unmolested … [this picket was] … surprised and taken by a party of fifteen or twenty militia who live on the road; but who had secreted themselves in the woods on our approach, and were advised of all our movements and positions by the women who are thronging around us on our march. Some of these men, I am informed, have been in our camp professing friendship …
> — General Porter to General Brown, July 16, 1814[22]

Porter's troops went further in their reprisals by burning the small village of St. Davids on July 18. This incident took place when a force of New York State Militia (Lieutenant Colonel Stone) and Willcock's renegade Canadian Volunteers became engaged in a skirmish with some Canadian militia pickets. While Stone and his militia were engaged beyond the village, the destructive fires began behind them and, according to Stone, happened without his knowledge or orders. The figure of suspicion obviously rested upon the Canadian Volunteers; nonetheless, in light of the previous year's embarrassing political debacle over the burning of Newark and the more recent British protestations over the similar destruction of civilian property at Port Dover and vicinity, General Brown responded with alacrity. Openly condemning the wanton act of destruction, he held Lieutenant Colonel Stone ultimately responsible and liable for dismissal from the army, a sentence that was rapidly and publicly enacted. Interestingly, this attitude toward these American excesses was not restricted to General Brown:

> The militia and Indians plundered and burnt everything. The whole population is against us: not a foraging party but is fired on, and not unfrequently returns with missing numbers. This state was to be anticipated. The militia have burnt … the village of St Davids … and my battalion was sent to cover the retreat as it was presumed they might be pursued. My God, what a service! I never witnessed such a scene, and had not the

commanding officer of the party, Lieut-Colonel Stone been disgraced and sent out of the army, I would have resigned ...
— Major MacFarland, Twenty-Third Regiment, July 17, 1814[23]

On July 20, General Brown's problems were compounded by the wholesale defection of his Native allies back to the U.S. side of the Niagara River. This unexpected departure was the result of the American warriors concluding a mutual non-aggression pact with their British Native counterparts from the Grand River region, leading to the removal of most of the region's Native warriors from both armies. Inevitably, the departure of these irregular troops led to some rapid recalculations of logistics and strategy on the part of General Brown and on the other side of the lines held by General Riall at Twenty Mile Creek. Nevertheless, General Brown's determination to hold the Lake Ontario waterfront in order to be able to meet up with the now suspiciously overdue Chauncey, plus Brown's decided intention of reducing and capturing the British forts, led him to order the destruction of all defence works at Queenston Heights and the movement of his army from Queenston to the outskirts of Newark (Niagara-on-the-Lake). Here his army began to establish a new camp and positions for

gun emplacements in front of what used to be the American-built fortifications at Fort George.

This American movement alarmed the British fort's commander, Lieutenant Colonel Tucker, especially when he also saw the Americans begin construction of new artillery emplacements at Youngstown, opposite Fort George. Once these emplacements were completed, it would place Fort George between two sets of fire and would inevitably lead to the loss of the position; which in turn would threaten the security of the other two forts. He therefore called upon General Riall to bring forward his troops and engage the enemy as soon as possible. Back at Twenty Mile Creek, this new information placed General Riall in an equally awkward position.

> I am really in a very unpleasant predicament. It will be expected that I should do something to relieve Fort George, which I certainly have every inclination to do, but if I advance from this [Twenty Mile Creek], I leave the country in my rear perfectly exposed to the enemy's advance from Queenston, or if I move in that direction and from thence to Fort George, the enemy may, if he pleases, detach a part of his force by the cross roads [Virgil] to effect the object of getting into

my rear and to Burlington. If besides, I
should advance and any reverse happen,
I look upon it as fraught with the greatest
danger to the province …
— Riall to Drummond, July 20, 1814[24]

Fortunately, by this time General Drummond
had recognized the necessity of taking over personal command of the army on the Niagara frontier
and was on his way from Kingston to York with
additional troops.

Meanwhile, despite having brought his army
before the forts and invested significant effort in
the construction of fieldworks and siege batteries,
General Brown soon saw that laying siege to the
British positions was beyond his means without
the heavy guns (that he still believed Chauncey was
going to deliver) to demolish the defensive works.
According to several of Brown's subordinates, including Major Jesup, commanding the Twenty-Fifth
Regiment, this conclusion was self-evident before
the move was made. As he later recorded:

The writer [Jesup] could never understand the object in moving to Fort
George. Our force was not sufficient to
warrant an attack, particularly when
General Rial, with a force known to be
nearly equal to ours was in the field. We

should have sought and beat him first
and then we might have taken the fort at
our leisure…but we allowed the moment
to pass and were consequently during
the remainder of the campaign, thrown
upon the defensive …[25]

Without either sign or news of Chauncey, and
with the campaign effectively stalled, Brown decided
that his only recourse was to shorten his supply lines
and establish himself in a strong defensive position.
He therefore ordered his forces to abandon their
new lines and retire upon Queenston once more.
On July 22, the American force began its march
south, only to find that a strong party of British
regulars and Canadian militia had occupied the still
smouldering remnants of the Americans' former
defensive positions. Seeking to envelop and capture
this enemy force by a swift movement on both flanks,
the American plan of action soon degenerated into
a confusing series of skirmishes that occupied the
rest of the day and stretched from Queenston to the
ruins of St. Davids. Eventually, the forces of General
Porter's militia and Captain Harris's cavalry succeeded in forcing the British/Canadian contingent
to retire, and the American army encamped once
again on the heights above Queenston.

The following morning, the answer to Brown's
question of "Where is Chauncey?" arrived in a

letter from General Gaines at Sackets Harbor — and it did not contain good news. Commodore Chauncey had reputedly been ill and had steadfastly refused to give his subordinates permission to venture out onto the lake to challenge Yeo's blockade of the eastern end of Lake Ontario. Furthermore, in addition to the fact that Chauncey was making it openly known that his first priority was to beat Sir James Yeo and his squadron and not to be a convenient transport carrier for the army, the commodore was also stating that as far as he was concerned no arrangement or specific rendezvous for July 10 had ever been arranged or agreed upon.

As if this was not bad enough, Gaines also reported that part of the large force of riflemen and artillery reinforcements (Major Morgan) that had been waiting for transportation to the Niagara frontier on Chauncey's vessels had attempted to make their own passage in small boats, only to run afoul of bad weather and the British naval patrols. Consequently, they had been forced to return to Sackets Harbor to await further orders.

Reading this, Brown's hopes of sweeping around the head of the lake to capture York and then Kingston evaporated. Furthermore, the essential artillery, supplies, and reinforcements at Sackets Harbor would now have to make the long and tiring journey overland — that is, if they came at all.

During a subsequent meeting with his senior commanders, the question of how to continue the campaign was discussed. General Brown stated he was now prepared to follow Ripley's original advice and seek out Riall's forces, or otherwise make a move toward Burlington along the rough trackways that ran across the top edge of the Niagara Escarpment. This proposal was vigorously endorsed by Winfield Scott to the point that he was prepared to see the American forces divide, even if it meant engaging the British forces on two fronts simultaneously. By contrast, Ripley was now not so keen on the idea, as his original plan had been based upon an advantage of the moment and he was well aware that in the intervening week the British had received substantial reinforcements, with more coming. Without any unified support to make a decision, Brown uncharacteristically went against the advice of Scott and vetoed any prospect of dividing his forces, a position that did not please Scott. In fact, Brown's subsequent accounts recorded, "He [Scott] appeared very tenacious on this subject and seemed vexed that the commanding General [Brown] would not consent to divide his force …"[26]

In fact, instead of returning the campaign to an offensive operation, General Brown decided his only option was to further shorten his existing supply line with Buffalo by retiring to the Chippawa River, there to place himself in a position where he could man-oeuvre according to the tactical situation and prepare a new plan of campaign. To this end, he issued the order to have the entire army retire and relieve itself of all encumbrances and superfluous baggage.

It must be evident to every reflecting and observing officer that this army is too much encumbered with baggage so as to retard its movements.... Therefore, in order to retain its full and entire strength, to be able to act with promptness and to move with alacrity ... the baggage will be reduced as follow, to wit;

1 Wall tent for each officer and 1 Common tent for the several waiters of the field officers of any regiment or battalion; to the officers of each company, when not exceeding three, one W[all] tent, if more than three, the addition of one C[ommon] tent, and for every ten Non-com, musicians, and privates, one C[ommon] tent, 1 C[ommon] kettle, one tin pan.

As regards to private baggage of officers, commandants of brigades or corps seeing the necessity, as they must, will exercise their ingenuity in curtailing it as far as practicable. This surplus baggage will immediately be collected ... where it will be sent ... to Buffalo. At the solicitation of the surgeons of the 9th and 23rd Regiments, one woman is permitted to be retained in each as hospital matrons. Surgeons of other regiments if they deem it necessary will do the same ...
— General Brown, General Order, July 23, 1814[27]

During this same period, General Drummond had arrived at York, along with the brigs *Star* and *Charwell*, which were packed with provisions. These were soon followed by several bateaux, equally filled with desperately needed supplies. While this temporarily eased the crisis of finding food to feed the army, the dependent militia families, and refugee Natives, Drummond knew it was only a short-term solution and that the issue was not going to disappear. Furthermore, the need to have the various Upper Canada militia regiments embodied for action and on campaign denied these men the opportunity of tending to their farms and gathering the approaching harvest. As a result, the longer the campaign continued, the worse his local supply situation would become, unless he weakened his fighting strength by allowing these militiamen to return to their homes.

After reviewing General Riall's latest reports on the activities of the Americans around Fort George, and not yet apprised of the American retreat to Queenston and then Chippawa, Drummond concluded that the new batteries being erected at Youngstown represented a significant threat to his defences at Fort George and Fort Mississauga. He therefore decided to go to Niagara himself and personally supervise a strong sortie from Fort Niagara to eliminate this threat and then press on to Lewiston and even Fort Schlosser, thus cutting Brown's supply lines. In preparation, he sent detailed instructions to Lieutenant Colonel Tucker at Fort George to prepare his troops for action in conjunction with a simultaneous movement by General Riall.

It is not Lieut-General Drummond's wish to risque an action on the left [west] bank of the river until the arrival of part of the reinforcements, which are marching on this place [York] … Should your attack on the right [east bank] be successful, the impression which it may occasion on the force of the enemy on this [west] side, particularly if his boats are gained by us, may afford a favourable opportunity, upon which the Major General is directed to improve, or in the case of failure … you are to move out every man who can be spared from the three forts and favour the Major General's

operations by threatening or attacking the enemy's rear.

— Lieutenant Colonel Harvey (for Drummond) to Lieutenant Colonel Tucker, York, July 23, 1813[28]

At the same time, Drummond wanted to ensure that Brown would be unable to send troops back across the Niagara River to counter this sortie. To this end, he sent Riall orders instructing him to advance his light brigade as a display of force toward the enemy to keep Brown's attention on the west bank of the river. Recognizing Riall's apparent hesitancy to engage the enemy after his defeat at Chippawa, Drummond included a set of specific directions on how Riall should place his troops should they come to battle with the Americans before he arrived to take charge. This letter was to have considerable influence on the British disposition of troops when the two armies finally came to blows two days later.

In order to favour … [Tucker's sortie] … and to draw the attention of the enemy from that side of the river … march to St Davids and concentrate the whole of the regular force under your command at that place, throwing the militia and Indians into the woods towards the enemy's

DISTRIBUTION OF BRITISH FORCES, JULY 8, 1814[*12]

Fort Niagara (Lieutenant Colonel Tucker — 41st Regiment)
Staff: 21
Royal Marine Artillery: 4 Officers, 68 Other Ranks
41st Regiment: 25 Officers, 513 Other Ranks
100th Regiment: 13 Other Ranks

Fort George (Lieutenant Colonel Gordon — 1st [Royal Scots] Regiment)
to Fort Mississauga (Major Evans — 8th [King's] Regiment):
19th Light Dragoons: 3 Officers, 71 Other Ranks, (plus) 4 Other Ranks sick/wounded*
Provincial Light Dragoons: 2 Officers, 18 Other Ranks
Royal Engineers: 2 Officers
Royal Sappers and Miners: 6 Other Ranks
Royal Artillery: 8 Officers, 168 Other Ranks, 2 Other Ranks sick/wounded*
Incorporated Militia Artillery: 1 Officer, 12 Other Ranks
Royal Artillery Drivers: 1 Officer, 32 Other Ranks, 2 Other Ranks sick/wounded
1st (Royal Scots) Regiment: 29 Officers, 801 Other Ranks, 153 Other Ranks sick/wounded*
8th (King's) Regiment: 27 Officers, 560 Other Ranks, 11 Other Ranks sick/wounded*
100th Regiment: 5 Officers, 293 Other Ranks, 121 Other Ranks sick/wounded*
Incorporated Militia: 33 Officers, 346 Other Ranks
Coloured Corps: 1 Officer, 25 Other Ranks, 4 Other Ranks sick/wounded

(* Principally composed of wounded from the Battle of Chippawa)

Long Point and Area (Lieutenant Colonel Parry — 103rd Regiment)
19th Light Dragoons: 3 Officers, 61 Other Ranks, 1 Other Ranks sick/wounded
Provincial Dragoons: 1 Officer, 13 Other Ranks
103rd Regiment: 12 Officers, 186 Other Ranks, 5 Other Ranks sick/wounded

Burlington Heights (Colonel H. Scott — 103rd Regiment)
Provincial Dragoons: 3 Other Ranks
Royal Artillery: 1 Officer, 3 Other Ranks
Royal Artillery Drivers: 1 Officer, 16 Other Ranks
103rd Regiment: 24 Officers, 658 Other Ranks, 27 Other Ranks sick/wounded

York: (Colonel Battersby — Glengarry Light Infantry)
Royal Artillery: 1 Officer, 11 Other Ranks
Royal Artillery Drivers: 1 Officer, 10 Other Ranks
Royal and Provincial Engineers: 1 Officer, 6 Other Ranks
1st (Royal Scots) Regiment: 1 Officer, 3 Other Ranks, 7 Other Ranks sick/wounded
8th (King's) Regiment: 2 Officers, 78 Other Ranks, 49 Other Ranks sick/wounded
41st Regiment: 2 Officers, 6 Other Ranks, 14 Other Ranks sick/wounded
89th Regiment: 1 Sergeant, 2 Other Ranks, 1 Other Ranks sick/wounded
103rd Regiment: 2 Other Ranks
Royal Newfoundland Regiment: 1 Officer, 2 Other Ranks
Glengarry Light Infantry: 18 Officers, 381 Other Ranks, 35 Other Ranks sick/wounded
Incorporated Militia: 1 Officer, 18 Other Ranks, 12 Other Ranks sick/wounded
Embodied Militia: 7 Officers, 6 Other Ranks, 6 Other Ranks sick/wounded

position and the lake…. This movement may be made with perfect safety on your part, as in event of the enemy's pushing … forward to attack or interpose betwixt you and Burlington, you can always … reach Shipman's before him, that is, provided you take precautions to cause his movements to be properly watched and reported…. Should the enemy by pressing suddenly and boldly on you make an action unavoidable, you must by means of the Glengarry Light Infantry and Incorporated Militia endeavour to check his light troops until you reach an open space in which, keeping your guns in your centre and your force concentrated, your flanks secured by light troops, Militia and Indians, you must depend upon the superior discipline of the troops under your command for success over an undisciplined though confident and numerous enemy …"

— General Drummond to
General Riall, July 23, 1814[29]

BRIGADES OF THE BRITISH RIGHT DIVISION, 16 JULY 1814[*20]

1st Brigade (Colonel Scott)
19th Light Dragoons (detachment)
8th (King's) Regiment
103rd Regiment
Royal Artillery (Three 6-pounder guns, 1 howitzer)

2nd Brigade (Lieutenant Colonel Pearson)
19th Light Dragoons (detachment)
Glengarry Light Infantry
Volunteer Battalion of Incorporated Militia
Royal Artillery (Two 6-pounder guns)

1st Militia Brigade (Lieutenant Colonel Perry)
1st / 2nd / 3rd / 4th / 5th Lincoln Militia Regiments

2nd Militia Brigade (Lieutenant Colonel Hamilton)
1st / 2nd Norfolk Militia Regiments
2nd York Militia Regiment

Reserve (Lieutenant Colonel Gordon)
1st (Royal Scots) Regiment

CHAPTER 3

The Roads to Battle, July 24–25, 1814

Having determined his course of campaign, Drummond shipped the 89th Regiment across the lake from York on July 24, 1814, agreeing with Riall's assessment that the town was in little danger of being attacked and that every man possible should be collected along the Niagara frontier. He then sailed aboard the schooner *Netley*, arriving the following morning at Newark.

Receiving a briefing, he was surprised to learn of the wholesale withdrawal of Brown's army to Chippawa and fully approved of General Riall's countermeasure of dispatching his light troops to shadow Brown's forces, while advancing his remaining forces to Ten Mile Creek. Recognizing that Brown's retreat created an opportunity of the moment, he ordered Lieutenant Colonel Tucker to immediately initiate his sortie from Fort Niagara and eliminate the enemy's batteries at Youngstown. Then, if not otherwise prevented, he was to push on to Lewiston and Fort Schlosser in order to capture Brown's supply boats, cutting off his supply lines.

At the same time, Drummond ordered the 89th Regiment (Lieutenant Colonel Morrison) and detachments from Fort George and Fort Mississauga to make a similar advance on the Canadian side of the river, while a small fleet of boats would maintain communications between the two forces under Captain Dobbs of the Royal Navy.

Advancing from Fort Niagara on the morning of July 25, 1814, Tucker's men quickly overran the Youngstown batteries and continued south to Lewiston, where they captured Brown's entire stockpile of "superfluous" baggage and tents that had

LOCATIONS AROUND THE LUNDY'S LANE HILLTOP AND PERSPECTIVES FOR THE FOLLOWING SEVEN IMAGES

1. Cook's Bog or "Muddy Run"
2. The Lundy's Lane church on the hilltop
3. Johnson's Tavern at the Lundy's Lane/Portage Road crossroad
4. Buchner farmstead
5. Forsyth's Tavern
6. Haggai Skinner's farmstead
7. Mrs. Wilson's tavern
8. Bridgewater Mills
9. Manchester, New York

A. View from the head of the whirlpool
B. Looking down the Niagara River toward Queenston
C. The Great Falls of Niagara, as seen from below Table Rock in 1801
D. The view of the Great Falls of Niagara from upriver at the hamlet of Bridgewater
E. Autumnal tints, road behind Lundy's Lane, Niagara Falls
F. Near Colonel Delatre's, a road parallel with Lundy's Lane, Niagara Falls
G. Part of a road between Stamford and Lundy's Lane

been laboriously transported across the river only the day before. Satisfied with this windfall, General Drummond called off the advance on Fort Schlosser and ordered Tucker to use part of his force to haul the captured goods back to Fort Niagara, while the remaining troops and Indians were ferried back across the Niagara River to Queenston.

View from the Head of the Whirlpool. Sir J.B.B. Estcourt, artist. An 1838 view of the spectacular Niagara River Gorge, below the falls (direction of view marked A on above map).

Looking Down the Niagara River Towards Queenston. Sir J.B.B. Estcourt, artist, 1838. (B)

Seven miles (11 kilometers) south of Queenston, Lieutenant Colonel Pearson's force had completed its overnight march from its base at Twelve Mile Creek, via the ruins of St. Davids, and arrived atop the rising ground that lay at the intersection of Lundy's Lane and Portage Road early on the bright, sunny morning of the twenty-fifth. Here they joined a party of Norton's Native warriors who had arrived the previous night. Sending out detachments of militia and Natives as scouts, Pearson's troops located the American pickets at the Chippawa, with their main encampment located just beyond the river. Secure in his position astride the two main trackways that controlled the north–south route between Chippawa and Queenston and the east–west route between the Great Falls and the interior road to Burlington, Pearson allowed his men to take a well-deserved rest. In response, the troops took up positions across the crest of the hill and for the remainder of the morning and well into the heat of the afternoon, they either dozed, cooked, or attended to the maintenance of their equipment and weapons, all the while keeping a watchful eye to the south with a strong screen of pickets composed of cavalry, militia, and Native allies.

Three miles (five kilometers) farther south, the American troops were also enjoying the fine weather by relaxing or attending to their own daily ritual of duties at their encampment, located on the south side of the Chippawa River where it flowed into the Niagara River. By noon, however, reports from their advanced pickets told of groups of British troops and Native warriors being seen around the widow Wilson's tavern on the road to Lundy's Lane and Queenston. Although not unduly concerned about this appearance of the enemy, Brown decided that an investigation was required and ordered

Lieutenant Riddle to cross the Chippawa with a detachment of about a hundred men from the Nineteenth Regiment in order to make a reconnaissance through the woods to the north and west of the American encampment. What was more alarming were the dispatches arriving from Colonel Swift at Lewiston reporting that a large force of British were rapidly advancing on that position and threatening to capture Brown's "surplus" supplies and baggage. This was followed by news from Captain Denman that the British had indeed captured Lewiston and were reported to be moving on his position at Fort Schlosser. Brown was now deeply concerned that a continuation of this British advance would not only

The Great Falls of Niagara, As Seen from below Table Rock in 1801. A.M. Hoffy, artist (after J. Vanderlyn), circa 1840. (C)

The View of the Great Falls of Niagara from Upriver at the Hamlet of Bridgewater. F.C. Christian, artist (after G. Heriot) 1807. The buildings in this image are the small residential/industrial complex known as Burch's Mill. (D)

Autumnal Tints, Road behind Lundy's Lane, Falls of Niagara. Lady C.B.B. Estcourt, artist, 1838. Looking east along what today is McCloud Road at Franklin Avenue, south of the hill. (E)

cut his supply lines from Fort Schlosser, but should the enemy advance on Buffalo, it would completely cut off his entire army. Brown was equally certain that if the British were making their main effort on the other side of the river, the troops being reported toward Lundy's Lane must only be a diversionary force, deliberately being exposed to keep him pinned in place while the main body took Fort Schlosser. This, ironically, was exactly what Drummond had originally planned.

Above: *Near Colonel Delatre's, A Road Parallel with Lundy's Lane, Niagara Falls.* Sir J.B.B. Estcourt, artist, 1838. Looking west along what today is Murray Street at its junction with Drummond Road, south of Lundy's Lane. (F)

(Right, above) *Part of a Road Between Stamford and Lundy's Lane.* Sir J.B.B. Estcourt, artist, 1838. A lane running up the northwest side of the hill toward Lundy's Lane. In 1814, this property was still just fields, with a fence running where the lane was later placed. This is also where the British forces assembled for their three major counterattacks. (G) (Right, below) The same perspective today. Drummond Road, looking south toward the hilltop crossing with Lundy's Lane. The churchyard is at the top of the hill and to the left.

By 2:00 p.m., General Brown decided to detach a part of General Porter's Third Brigade to cross back over the Niagara River to reinforce the vulnerable Fort Schlosser. At the same time, he ordered a strong probe be made on his own (west) side of the river by moving along the Portage Road toward Queenston

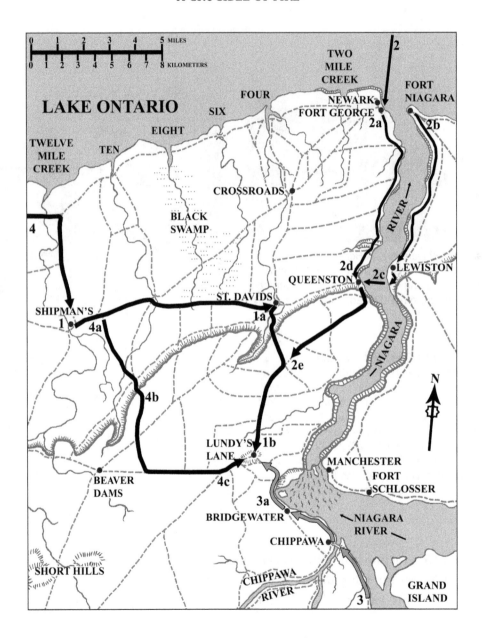

THE ROUTES TAKEN BY THE VARIOUS COMBATANT UNITS IN THEIR MARCH TO LUNDY'S LANE ON JULY 24–25, 1814

1. The British "light" brigade (1) leaves the 12 Mile Creek around 10:00 p.m. on July 24 and marches overnight, arriving at St. Davids around dawn (1a). It then marches on to the Lundy's Lane cross-roads and encamps on the hilltop at around 7:00 a.m. (1b).
2. General Drummond arrives at Newark (2) by ship from York around dawn of July 25. He orders a two-pronged advance up the Niagara River from Fort George (2a) on the British side and Fort Niagara (2b) on the American side. After over-running General Brown's baggage supplies at Lewiston, General Drummond's force crosses back to Queenston around noon (2c). After consulting with General Riall (2d), General Drummond orders an advance on Lundy's Lane (2e).
3. After receiving reports of a British advance on the American side of the river over the course of the day, General Brown orders General Scott's brigade to advance from camp (3) toward Lundy's Lane (3a) sometime after 4:00 p.m.
4. Colonel Hercules Scott's column (4) marches up from the Twenty Mile Creek to Shipman's Corners (St. Catharines) and halts early on the morning of July 25 (4a). At around 1:00 p.m., and upon receiving initial orders to rendezvous with Brown at Lundy's Lane, it advances toward the hill. Due to being diverted, as these orders are first counter-manded and then revoked, re-establishing the original destination, the exact route of this column is conjectural (4b) up to the Beaver Dams Road. From this point, the column advances toward the Lundy's Lane hilltop (4c), arriving at around 9:00 p.m., as the battle is already well underway.

and Fort George. With this countermeasure, Brown reasoned that since his defeat at Chippawa, General Riall had remained on the defensive (Brown was still unaware of Drummond's arrival) and this probe would cause Riall to abandon his advance on the east bank and retire on his forts to maintain their safety. Confident that only a part of the army would be required for this countermeasure, Brown chose Scott's brigade, supported by artillery and mounted troops, to undertake the advance along the Portage/Queenston Road. Their orders were to locate and report on British dispositions, and, if feasible, pressure Riall into withdrawing toward the river mouth — while the remaining American brigades were to remain at Chippawa.[*1]

Back at Queenston, the bulk of Drummond's forces had, by now, completed their recrossing of the Niagara River and the 41st and 100th Regiments marched north, back to Fort George and Fort Mississauga. In addition, General Riall arrived bearing news that Pearson's force was secure at Lundy's Lane with the Americans to the south at Chippawa. Discussing options with Riall, Drummond decided that the situation was opportune and ordered a concentration of units at the Lundy's Lane hilltop. Riall would rejoin Pearson and his advanced force, while Drummond was to follow with the remaining part of Lieutenant Colonel Morrison's column. Riders were also sent to order up Colonel Hercules

ESTIMATE OF AMERICAN FORCES, BATTLE OF LUNDY'S LANE, JULY 25, 1814[*1]

Strength, on paper, according to muster rolls: 5,009 All Ranks. According to Ripley's account (3,588 All Ranks, of which 2,997 were Rank and File)

Strength, fit for duty, according to muster rolls: 4,232 All Ranks, Ripley (2,990 All Ranks, 2,458 Rank and File)

Author's estimate of strength used in the battle (based on estimated deductions from the above for detached units at Buffalo, Fort Erie, Fort Schlosser, forces remaining in camp, and other units that are recorded as not joining the action): 2,500–2,800 All Ranks, Ripley (2,240 All Ranks, 1,779 Rank and File)

LEFT DIVISION (Major General Brown)

First Brigade (Brigadier General Winfield Scott)
Ninth Regiment (Major Leavenworth): 200 Rank and File
Eleventh Regiment (Major McNeil): 200 Rank and File
Twenty-Second Regiment (Colonel Brady): 300 Rank and File
Twenty-Fifth Regiment (Major Jesup): 380 Rank and File

Second Brigade (Brigadier General Ripley)
First Regiment (Lieutenant Colonel Nicholas): 150 Rank and File (detachment)
Twenty-First Regiment (Lieutenant Colonel Miller): 432 Rank and File*
Twenty-Third Regiment (Major McFarland): 300 Rank and File

Third Brigade (Brigadier General Porter)
New York State Militia (Lieutenant Colonel Dobbin): 250 Rank and File
Fifth Pennsylvania Militia (Major Wood): 246 Rank and File
Canadian Volunteers Regiment (Lieutenant Colonel Willcocks): 50 Rank and File

Artillery (Major Hindman)
Captain Biddle's Battery (Three 6-pounder guns)
Captain Ritchie's Battery (Two 6-pounder guns, One 5 ½ inch howitzer)
Captain Towson's Battery (Two 6-pounder guns, One 5 ½ inch howitzer)
Captain William's Battery (Three 18-pounder guns)**
Lieutenant Douglass's Battery (Two 18-pounder guns)**
Combined Total: 200 Gunners

Cavalry (Captain Harris)
U.S. Light Dragoons (Captain Harris): 1 Troop
New York State Militia Dragoons (Captain Broughton): volunteers
Combined Total: 70 All Ranks

(* Includes attached units, i.e., 1 company, Seventeenth Regiment (Captain Chunn), 1 company, Nineteenth Regiment (Lieutenant Riddle)
(** Not recorded as actively participating in the battle)

N.B. For additional details on these numbers see Notes.

Scott's brigade from the Twelve Mile Creek,[*2] thus placing the British in an advantageous position for a probable attack on the Americans the following day. Unfortunately, circumstances were to pre-empt this orderly plan and precipitate a battle of confusion and chaos in the darkness of the approaching night.

ESTIMATE OF BRITISH FORCES, BATTLE OF LUNDY'S LANE, JULY 25, 1814

(Lieutenant General Drummond)

RIGHT DIVISION (Major General Riall) AT LUNDY'S LANE

2nd (Light) Brigade (Lieutenant Colonel Pearson)
Infantry
Glengarry Light Infantry (Lieutenant Colonel Battersby): 376 Other Ranks
Incorporated Militia of Upper Canada (Lieutenant Colonel Robinson): 336 Other Ranks

Cavalry
19th Light Dragoons (Major Lisle): 95 Other Ranks
Provincial Light Dragoons (Captain Merritt): 30 Other Ranks

Artillery
Two 6-pounder guns, One 5 ½ inch howitzer
Total: 20 Crew

1st Militia Brigade (Lieutenant Colonel Parry)

1st / 2nd / 4th / 5th Lincoln Militias: detachments
2nd York Militia (Major Simons): detachment
Total: 300 Other Ranks

Native Allies (Captain Norton)
50 Warriors

MARCHED FROM FORT GEORGE AND FORT MISSISSAUGA

Fort Garrisons (Lieutenant Colonel Morrison)
Infantry
1st (Royal Scots) Regiment (Captain Brereton): detachment 171 Other Ranks
8th (King's) Regiment (Captain Campbell): detachment 65 Other Ranks
41st Regiment (Captain Glew): detachment 60 Other Ranks
89th Regiment (Lieutenant Colonel Morrison): 425 Other Ranks

Artillery
Two 24-pounder guns (Lieutenant Thomkyns/ Tomkyns)
Royal Marine Artillery, Congreve Rocket Section (Sergeant Austin)
Total: 40 Crew

Native Allies
(Unknown number)

MARCHED FROM TWELVE MILE CREEK

1st Brigade (Colonel Hercules Scott)

Infantry

1st (Royal Scots) Regiment (Lieutenant Colonel
    Gordon): detachment, 400 Other Ranks
8th (King's) Regiment (Major Evans): detachment,
    275 Other Ranks
103rd Regiment (Major Smelt): detachment, 635
    Other Ranks
104th Regiment (Captain Leonard): detachment,
    120 Other Ranks

Artillery

Three six 6-pounder guns (Captain Mackonochie):
    40 Other Ranks

2nd Militia Brigade (Lieutenant Colonel

Hamilton)

Infantry

1st / 2nd Norfolk Militias: detachments
1st Essex Militia: detachment
1st Middlesex Militia: detachment
Western (Caldwell's) Rangers: detachment
Estimated Total: 250 Other Ranks

CHAPTER 4

First Contact and the Race for the Hilltop

Although ready to march, General Scott delayed his departure, looking for news from Riddle's reconnaissance force. However, the advance screen of British pickets had forced Riddle to make a wide detour through the dense bush. Consequently, he took considerably longer than expected to reach a vantage point to study Pearson's troops on the hilltop. Furthermore, once in position, instead of remaining on watch and dispatching runners with ongoing reports of the enemy's activities back to his commander, Riddle ordered his entire unit to retrace their meandering route through the woods, thus leaving Scott and Brown unaware of what lay before them. Eventually, giving up on Riddle, Winfield Scott ordered the advance. To many of the troops in camp or along the riverbank washing clothes, the sight of Scott's brigade marching out in full kit as the day began to wane merely signified that the taskmaster was doing more of his never-ending drills. Even within the column, the consensus was that they were simply going out to secure the ground in front of the camp from the predatory attentions of an encroaching screen of enemy light troops. Advancing along the road that curved around the riverbank alongside the rapids and directly above the falls, the sight of increasing numbers of British pickets in the distance persuaded Scott that precautions needed to be taken. The Ninth Regiment was therefore detached from the column to cover its left flank in the dense woods. Consequently, the continued advance of the main column was slowed, as the two elements sought to maintain position with each other.

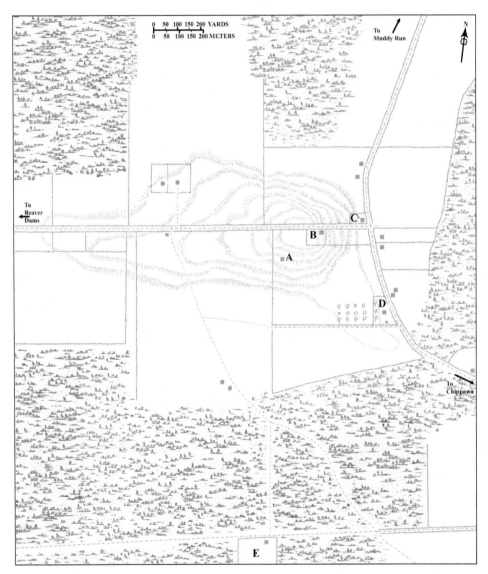

THE LUNDY'S LANE BATTLEFIELD IN 1814

A. Buchner house
B. Lundy's Lane churchyard
C. Johnson's Tavern, at the crossroads of Lundy's Lane (E–W) and Portage Road (N–S)
D. Pier's farmstead
E. Skinner's farmstead

Approaching Mrs. Wilson's tavern, which stood on a section of high ground that overlooked the falls, Scott and his entourage witnessed several British officers exiting the building.

We had proceeded nearly three-fourths of the distance from Chippawa to the Falls without any particular incident, when in passing round a small coppice of woods, we came in sight of an old dwelling-house, the residence of Mrs Wilson. There was a number of Cavalry-horses in the yard ... and almost at the instant our eyes fell on them, eight or ten British officers stepped hastily from the house and mounted their horses. Some of them rode away briskly; but three or four, after mounting, faced towards us and surveyed us with their glasses [telescopes]. An elderly officer of dignified and commanding mien stationed himself in the middle of the road, a little in advance of his companions, and coolly inspected the head of our column as it came in sight. They waited until we had approached within perhaps two hundred and fifty yards; and then retreated slowly, with their glasses scarcely withdrawn, until the leading officer, closing

his glass ... [gave] ... a military salute, which was promptly returned by us, as they all wheeled and rode swiftly away ...

— Douglass[1]

Reaching the tavern, Scott questioned Mrs. Wilson, who provided the general with a fairly accurate account of the significant strength of the British troops that lay beyond the next belt of trees. Openly sceptical of the woman's account, Scott now committed the first of what was to become a series of command errors made that night, as he let his preconceived judgment (that only a small force lay before him) overrule this valid intelligence. In his own words:

It seemed evident that there was a Corps of observation in the neighborhood, and Scott so reported to headquarters; but from the information on which he had advanced, it could only be a small body, detached from an inferior army that had committed the folly of sending at least half its numbers to the opposite side of the river ...

— Winfield Scott[2]

Nevertheless, he still took the precaution of sending Major Jones, his assistant adjutant general,

(Facing, above) An illustration from the *Canadian Illustrated News* for July 15, 1876. It shows the perspective of the Lundy's Lane hilltop from the south. Although done at a significantly later date and including both roads established after the war and the extensive subdivision of previously larger field lots, it still retains an idea of the ground, long since obliterated by the wholesale sweep of urban development. (Facing, below) A duplicate image with locations linked to the battle highlighted and marked.

An illustration from the *Canadian Illustrated News* for July 15, 1876.

A. Buchner house
B. Lundy's Lane churchyard
C. Johnson's Tavern, at the crossroads of Lundy's Lane (L-L) and Portage Road (P-P)
D. Pier's farmstead

Dr. Post-war development of the line of the current-day Drummond Road
Cu. Post-war development of the line of the current-day Culp Street
O. Post-war observation towers, providing tourists with a panoramic view of the battlefield

with a report to General Brown but without asking for reinforcements, as he obviously considered he could deal with the matter himself.

As Captain Harris's dragoons and the advance guard of the American column approached the woods to the north, they came under fire from a small party of British Native allied warriors and began to take casualties. Pushing forward, the American advance cleared the intervening woodland and entered the fields beyond. From here they could plainly see British formations moving across the hilltop and guns being positioned some seven hundred yards (640 meters) ahead. Galloping back, a wounded dragoon messenger notified General Scott of what really lay ahead. Still confident of his ability to contend with the forces before him, Scott made no effort to make a personal reconnaissance before committing his troops, choosing instead to continue with the advance, while sending a further report to Brown — only this time looking for support.

Calling together his regimental and unit commanders, Scott held a briefing that would see the Ninth Regiment re-form as the head of the column, with the Twenty-Second and Eleventh falling in behind. Their orders were to advance along the road into the clear fields ahead and then deploy to the left of the road in succession of regiments (which would place the Ninth on the right and the Eleventh on the far left of the line), while the artillery would be positioned along the road itself. The Twenty-Fifth Regiment was detached, as it had been at Chippawa, to act independently on the right of the main column and attempt to turn the enemy's flank.

Having watched the Twenty-Fifth move off into the woods, Scott took his place at the head of the column and led it confidently forward.

Within moments, the leading files moved out from the shelter of the road, which ran like a corridor through the woods. Looking toward the rising ground before him, Scott was shocked to see that the British force arrayed against him was not only far greater than he had assumed, but was also well beyond the numbers quoted by both Mrs. Wilson and the dragoon messenger. The reason for this increase was, however, easily explained and lay in the fact that Scott's cumulative delays had allowed the British just enough time to receive reinforcements and get their troops back into position, after previously abandoning it upon hearing of the initial American advance.

This confusing scramble for position had begun earlier in the day as Pearson's light troops relaxed on the Lundy's Lane hilltop and began preparations for their evening meal. As the afternoon progressed, an increasing number of reports of American troop movements had reached General Riall. This culminated in the return of the officers from Mrs. Wilson's tavern, who notified him of the approaching American column. Remembering his overconfident assumptions at Chippawa and certain that Brown would not make the foolish mistake of dividing his forces and only sending one brigade against him (which of course he had!), Riall believed himself to be facing the entire American army on the march. He therefore

The Lundy's Lane battlefield churchyard in 2013.

(Facing, top) The view from the position taken by the British artillery battery.

(A) British artillery position.
(B) The direction of the Great Falls and the direction from which Miller's attack approached the hill.
(C-D) The line of the Portage Road that comes from Chippawa (C) and runs off to the left (D) toward the crossroads with Lundy's Lane.
(E) The direction in which Scott's brigade formed its line and advanced toward the hill.

(Facing, middle) The view of the hilltop from a position directly south of the British artillery position.

(A) British artillery position.
(E) Estimate of where Scott's First Brigade was consolidated into a single formation.

(Facing bottom) The view of the hilltop from the perspective of Miller's force (B) as it advanced up toward the British artillery position (A).

decided to withdraw toward Queenston in order to join up with Drummond and Morrison's force. Together they could then give battle, or at least stall the Americans long enough to allow Hercules Scott's column to arrive and tip the balance in their favour. Dispatching a message directing Hercules Scott's column to move on Queenston and not Lundy's Lane, Riall ordered the retreat of Pearson's

brigade. Calling in the remaining pickets and packing their food and cooking implements, Pearson's troops limbered up their guns and formed a column, before leaving the hilltop and marching north along the road for Queenston. The hill now stood bare and free for the taking, but Winfield Scott was still well up the road at Wilson's Tavern and not ready to advance — and his window of opportunity was narrowing.

Led by the embodied militia regiments and Native allies, Riall's column next consisted of his supply wagons and artillery, followed by the detachment of cavalry, the Incorporated Militia, and the Glengarry Light Infantry as rearguard. However, before the column had gone more than two miles north, it reached the lowland swampy area known as Cook's Bog — or the more descriptive "Muddy Run." Here it came face to face with Morrison's column,

THE INITIAL MOVEMENTS AND RELATIVE POSITIONS OF THE TWO ARMIES (CIRCA 5:00–6:45 P.M.)

(*N.B.* The timings indicated in the following maps represent the current use of eastern daylight (EDT) summertime hours, i.e., with the addition of one hour, compared to the timings recorded in the original accounts. Sunset would therefore have occurred around 7:45 p.m. in the original timeline and 8:45 p.m. by these timings. In addition, due to the lack of any standardized time in 1814 and the variations of timings given in original accounts as individuals from the two armies set their own clocks independently, the timings should also be given a leeway of plus or minus 30 minutes.)

A. Buchner house
B. Lundy's Lane churchyard
C. Johnson's Tavern, at the crossroads of Lundy's Lane (E–W) and Portage Road (N–S)
D. Pier's farmstead

1. Following its meeting with General Drummond's column at Muddy Run, Pearson's retiring "light" brigade (1) moves back to the Lundy's Lane hilltop at the double-quick pace, cutting across the open fields. Arriving at the hilltop, the Incorporated Militia (IMUC) (1a) forms its line on the left (east) side of the hill, while the Glengarry Light Infantry (GLI) (1b) deploys in line to the right (west) side. The light brigade artillery (1c) moves up Portage Road and Lundy's Lane before unlimbering on the crest of the hill at the edge of the cemetery.

2. The embodied militias (2) and Native allies (2a) advance across the fields to take up positions on the far right (west) of the British line. The 19th Light Dragoons and militia cavalry detachment (2b) move up ahead of Drummond's still-advancing column (2c, 2d) and take up a covering position near the crossroads.

3. The U.S. cavalry detachment (3) and infantry advanced guard (3a) hold their initial reconnaissance positions on Portage Road and at the south end of the open ground, near Pier's farm. The leading element of General Winfield Scott's First Brigade column (3b) advances up the Portage Road from Chippawa.

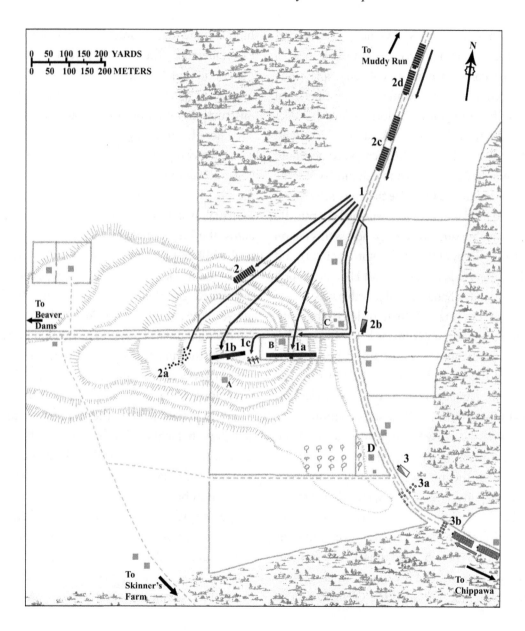

arriving from Queenston with General Drummond. Halting the retreating force, Drummond held a momentary conference with Riall and, according to some accounts, took the time to make a personal inspection from the hilltop before making his decision to reclaim the hill and make a defensive stand against the Americans. He also recognized he would have to redirect Hercules Scott's column back to its rendezvous at Lundy's Lane. He therefore selected an experienced local militia officer, who had an intimate knowledge of the paths and byways across this region (Major James Kerby of the Incorporated Militia), and gave him orders to locate and escort Hercules Scott's column to Lundy's Lane with all possible speed.

General Drummond then ordered the combined force in Muddy Run back to the Lundy's Lane hilltop. Because several days of heavy rains had turned the ground on either side of the road into an aptly named "muddy" quagmire, the only practical way of returning Pearson's column to the hill was to have every unit simply turn around and march back whence they came. This was a simple manoeuvre for the infantry, but for the more cumbersome wagons and artillery, turning around would be more difficult in the restricted space available. Determined to get his forces onto the hilltop as soon as possible and thus deny the enemy the strategic advantage of holding the high ground, General Drummond ordered the Glengarry Light Infantry and Incorporated Militia, who were not encumbered by the offending vehicles, to move at the double-quick back to the hill and hold back the Americans until the remaining units could clear the obstructions and move up to extend the position.

Literally running back the way they had just come, the companies composing the two regiments began to fan out, each taking their own path across the obstructed fields. As a result, they engaged in a virtual steeplechase race as they cut diagonally across the fences and fields before reaching the crest of the hill and forming their line of battle. On the left were the companies of the Incorporated Militia, positioned on the eastern slope of the hilltop between the chapel and the Portage Road crossroad. On the right, the Glengarries formed on the western slope of the hill. Shortly thereafter, the light brigade's artillery arrived and immediately unlimbered their guns, precisely where they had been only a couple of hours before, at the boundary of the small cemetery that marked the crest of the hill of Lundy's Lane. This was then followed by the detachments of embodied militia, but only part of the Native force — who now became divided in their commitment to fight an engagement in the white man's fashion, that being in such an open and exposed position. As a result, some of the warriors remained on the hillside, while the remainder moved down the slope to support the Glengarries on the right flank.

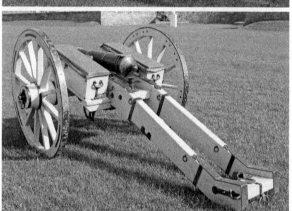

Left: A British 6-pounder artillery piece. Note the ready-use ammunition magazines strapped to the cross axle on either side of the barrel. Weapons of this calibre were used by both sides in the battle and represented the "standard" field-gun for their artillery, with a barrel length of approximately 8 feet (2.4 meters). Depending on whether the barrel was bronze or iron, the combined weight of this piece, without any additional limber or ammunition, would still reach an exhausting range of 3,600–3,800 pounds (1,633–1,724 kilos). In comparison, the two brass-barrel 24-pounder guns used by the British that night would have each weighed in at around 8,000–8,500 pounds (3,629–3,856 kilos).

Below: An American 5 ½ inch howitzer and associated limber. Artillery of this type and calibre was also used by both sides at Lundy's Lane. The combined weight of this "lighter" piece and its limber would still be approximately 2,000 pounds (907 kilos).

As successive units arrived on the field, General Drummond applied the guidelines he had previously laid out for General Riall for the disposition of his forces and drew up his regulars in a solid line, placed behind the crest of the hill and directly behind the junction of the Glengarry Light Infantry and Incorporated Militia. He then

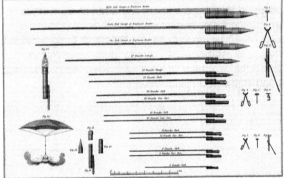

Illustrations taken from an instruction manual for the Congreve rocket system. (Above) Firing in the field from launching ramps constructed of a ladder with supporting poles and brackets. (Below) The range of rockets that was available in the Congreve arsenal of projectiles.

at the main crossroads to the east of the hill, supported by the troop of 19th Light Dragoons.

According to Lieutenant Duncan Clark of the Incorporated Militia:

> The Incorporated Militia formed the left of the line, a wood on their left and a buckwheat field between them and another wood in their front. The 89th Regiment were on their right on the brow of the hill and detachments of the Royals, 8th, 104th and 41st Regts formed the right of the line. The Glengarry Fencibles and militia were in a wood in advance of the British right ...[3]

Ensign John Kilborn, also of the Incorporated Militia, recorded:

> Our regiment was on the left of the line from the main road to the river, which was skirted by a strip of woods.... About three quarters of a mile below the Falls, the Glengarry, 85th Regiment, and detachments [from other regiments] were formed from the main road on our right, up Lundy's Lane where our artillery was posted, the ground rising in that direction ...[4]

ordered the two colonial regiments to march outward from each other, thus creating a gap in the centre, into which he inserted his regulars, while keeping his light troops on the flanks. In addition, as further artillery teams arrived, they were directed to join the battery on the hilltop, while a small Congreve rocket detachment from the Royal Marine Artillery Regiment set up their position

American artillery in action at Living History re-enactments of the War of 1812–1815.

Surprised but gratified to have regained the position on the hilltop without opposition, the troops looked to the south, fully expecting to see the enemy formed in the fields before them. Instead, apart from some enemy cavalry skirmishers, the anticipated formations of American infantry and artillery were only now coming into view, marching down the road from Chippawa.

Repeatedly delayed in its advance, General Scott's column had now missed its opportunity to capture the important road junction and strategic hilltop without a fight. Instead, looking toward the hilltop and having previously been assured by General Brown that only a small diversionary detachment was in the vicinity, General Scott was now confronted by an enemy line that stretched across the entire crest of the hill, outflanking him on both sides and consisting of considerably more troops than he had believed could possibly be in the area. Scott was now faced with the unenviable choice of retiring his force toward the cover of the woods and calling for reinforcements, or continuing forward and engaging a strong force of the enemy in a solid defensive position. Being the

THE AMERICAN LINE DEPLOYS, AS THE BRITISH SOLIDIFY THEIR POSITION ON THE HILLTOP (CIRCA 7:00–7: 30 P.M.)

A. Buchner house
B. Lundy's Lane churchyard
C. Johnson's Tavern
D. Pier's farmstead

1. In the British line, the IMUC (1) moves left (east) and takes up a position as the far left of the developing British line (1a). The GLI (1b) initially mirrors this move by shifting to the right (west) (1c). It then advances (south) and extends into a "light" infantry formation (1d). The embodied militias (1e) also advance down the west side of the hill in line, while the Native contingent divides, with part remaining on the hill (1f) and the remainder moving down the slope (1g).
2. Additional units from General Drummond's column, composed of a detachment of the 1st (Royal Scots) (2), the 89th Regiment (2a), a detachment of the 8th (King's) (2b), arrive on the field and take up positions in the line.
3. The Royal Marine Congreve Rocket Detachment (3) arrives at the crossroads and deploys in the grounds of Johnson's Tavern (C). In response, the British cavalry detachments move right (west) to provide support by occupying the crossroads (3a). Threatened by the back-blast of the rockets, the 89th Regiment (3b) retires its left wing. Additional artillery from General Drummond's column (3c) arrives and deploys on the crest of the hill. A detachment of the 41st Regiment (3d) arrives on the field as the action commences.
4. The U.S. cavalry detachment (4) advances to cover the movement and deployment of General Winfield Scott's First Brigade (4a) to the west of the Portage Road. A battery of U.S. artillery (Towson's) (4b) unlimbers alongside the road and commences fire at the hilltop.
5. General Scott's column (5) moves off the road to the left (west) to deploy into line and comes under heavy artillery fire from the hilltop. The Ninth Regiment (5a) remains relatively unscathed and deploys into line. However, the Twenty-Second (5b) suffers casualties and routs through the Eleventh Regiment (5c), causing a cascade rout (5d) without any of the American infantry units yet having fired a shot.
6. The Twenty-Fifth Regiment (6), previously detached with orders to move through the forest toward the British left flank, advances unseen through the woods in file.

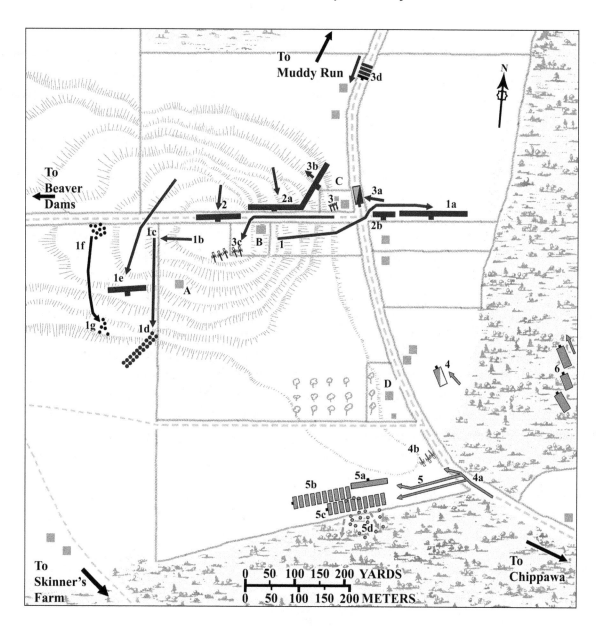

commander that he was, Winfield Scott chose to continue the advance. Entering the open fields and swinging off to the left of the road, the First Brigade's column began its deployment into line. According to Colonel Leavenworth, commanding officer of the Ninth Regiment:

> The enemy commenced firing upon us [with] artillery, two of which were 24 pounders and within cannister distance. They also opened at the same time a brisk fire upon us from a heavy line of Inf'y posted to the right and obliquely in front of their artillery. After advancing into the field … Gen'l Scott ordered "Form Line to Front" this order was immediately executed by the [Ninth Regiment by the] eschellon movement of companies to the left. The 22nd and 11th regiments moved in column until gaining their respective distances & formed line in the same manner at about the same time. The company of artillery … was moved up & formed on the right of the 9th Reg't.[5]

Unfortunately, this officer's perspective, being with the leading regiment in the column, was somewhat limited and he failed to recount what was actually happening to the units farther back in the column. There, forced to surmount a sturdy split-rail fence that lay in their path to the left, the troops of the Twenty-Second and Eleventh either battered the obstacle to the ground or climbed over it, thus losing much of their regimental cohesion, which was compounded by the heavy fire from the British guns on the hilltop. According to a later deposition, made by Major John McNeil of the Eleventh Regiment,

> The 11th wheeled on the left, nearly forming a right angle with the 22nd regiment; when the 11th was in the act of wheeling, the 22nd broke and ran athwart the 11th and broke several platoons considerably to pieces. I was a little in front of where the breach took place … and wheeled my horse in order to collect the men if possible, but the bushes being so near they gained them, which made it impracticable for me to perform that duty …[6]

CHAPTER 5

The Battle of Lundy's Lane, July 25, 1814: Stand and Fight

Despite having just seen his brigade's fighting formation disrupted at the very onset of the action and without having fired a shot, Winfield Scott was still determined to engage the enemy. Detaching several junior officers and sergeants to retrieve the fleeing men, Scott ordered the remaining officers of the First Brigade to form their remaining troops into a shortened line, with the intention of firing on the British. Stationed at a distance of between five hundred and six hundred yards (457–548 meters), the main enemy line was still beyond double the most optimistic range of the muskets carried by the troops in Scott's force. However, instead of advancing to close the distance and engage the British line directly, Scott allowed his troops to remain in that exposed position for more than thirty minutes, firing volleys that could not have possibly inflicted any casualties and only succeeded in wasting ammunition.

It has been argued amongst historians over the past two hundred years that Scott made this decision in order to retrieve his previously absconded troops, or that he was hoping that Riall would repeat the error of judgment he made at Chippawa by leaving his best defensible position and advancing to the attack. Irrespective of the reason, the reality was that the American line now presented a perfect target to the artillery on the hilltop and consequently took the full brunt of the British gunfire. Meanwhile, increasing numbers of the Glengarry Light Infantry, embodied militias, and Norton's Native warriors soon came into range and prowled the line of fencing and woods off to the left of the American line. Together these units sent in a steady

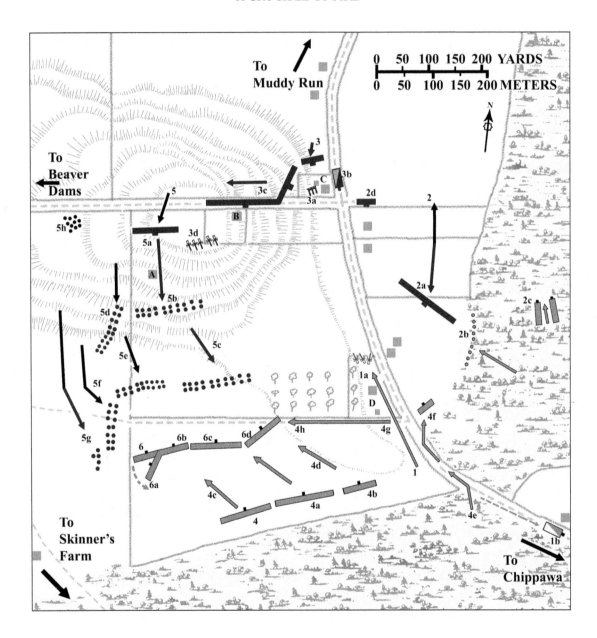

THE AMERICAN FIRST BRIGADE ENGAGES THE BRITISH RIGHT FLANK (CIRCA 7:30–8:30 P.M.)

A. Buchner house
B. Lundy's Lane churchyard
C. Johnson's Tavern
D. Pier's farmstead

1. Unable to effectively engage the British guns on the hill, Towson's artillery (1) advances to a new position (1a) at Pier's farmstead (D) while the U.S. cavalry detachments (1b) leave the field.
2. Considering Towson's American artillery (1a) to be a target of opportunity, the Incorporated Militia (2) advances from the left flank of the British line in an attempt to outflank the guns (2a), but then comes under fire from both the artillery and part of the Twenty-Fifth Regiment (2b) hiding within the wood line to the east. The remainder of the Twenty-Fifth (2c) continues to move north through the woods. Under fire from two flanks, the Incorporated Militia retires to its original position alongside the 8th (King's) Regiment (2d).
3. The detachment of the 41st Regiment (3) arrives at the line and takes up a position behind the Congreve rockets (3a) and cavalry detachments (3b). This allows the 89th Regiment (3c) to move to the right (west) to better cover the artillery (3d) on the hilltop.
4. General Winfield Scott's First Brigade: Eleventh (4), Twenty-Second (4a), and Ninth (4b) Regiments, deploy into line and open fire, but at too great a range to fire effectively on the main British line on the hilltop. It remains static for over half an hour, thereby suffering severe casualties from the British artillery fire. Eventually, the line is ordered to advance to the left (4c, 4d). At the same time, elements of the previously broken column are rallied (4e), and after moving onto the road and then deploying to the right (west) of the road (4f), are ordered to rejoin the line (4g, 4h).
5. In response to the American advance, the 1st (Royal Scots) Detachment (5) is initially moved forward (south) in line (5a) and then advance to the foot of the hill in light infantry formation (5b, 5c) to engage the American line from the front. This advance is supported by a similar advance by the GLI (5d, 5e), embodied militias (5f), and Native allies (5g), who succeed in outflanking the American left flank. On the hill, the remaining element of the Native allies remains uncommitted (5h).
6. Responding to the British flanking threat, the American line is halted and the Eleventh Regiment's left flank (6) swings back (6a) to engage the British infantry on the left (5e–5f). The right wing of the Eleventh (6b) and Twenty-Second Regiments (6c) engage the units to its front (5c, 5e). The combined Ninth Regiment and re-formed detachments (6d) wheel forward to the left and open fire shortly before the remainder of the line begins to run out of ammunition, while all units are continuing to suffer casualties from the British infantry fire and the British artillery on the hilltop.

fusillade of fire that inflicted an increasing number of casualties within the ranks of the Eleventh Regiment, while their return fire proved substantially ineffective against the hidden Canadians and Natives. It was only on the right, where Towson had unlimbered his guns, that any counter-fire could reach the main British line. But here, too, there was a problem, for the position of the British guns on the higher ground prevented the American battery from elevating their guns sufficiently to do any significant damage. Frustrated at this difficulty, Towson's battery ceased fire, limbered up, and moved down the Portage Road. Here they set up a new firing position within the orchard of the Pier farmstead, at the foot of the slope from the top of which the British guns were systematically pounding the First Brigade into extinction.

Within the main American line, the British artillery fire tore holes in the ranks and caused particularly heavy casualties at the points where the large regimental colours (flags) were placed. This is not surprising as these rallying symbols were not only where the senior officers were located, but as they stuck out of the clouds of smoke produced by the volleys of fire, they also provided an ideal aiming point for the British gunners. Consequently, most of the senior officers of the First Brigade's regiments were either killed or wounded in this initial bombardment.

At the same time, off to the right, the cavalry detachment and artillery likewise suffered casualties — to the point where Captain Harris withdrew his light dragoons from the field.

Despite seeing his brigade being destroyed around him, Scott refused to contemplate retiring to the woods to await reinforcements. Instead, he decided to attack the British right flank. Sending another message to Brown (this time calling for immediate assistance), Scott ordered the advance. In response, the dogged determination of the troops showed itself and the hours of drill served their purpose as the survivors of the First Brigade line stepped over the bodies of their fallen comrades and closed on their colours as they moved forward and to the left, heading for the British infantry visible on the western flank of the hill.

During this same period and on the eastern side of the battlefield, a separate conflict was being fought between Major Jesup's Twenty-Fifth Regiment and the Canadian regiment of the Incorporated Militia. After moving out from the main column toward the British left flank, Jesup's force had come across a small track that allowed them to move through the dense woods and hopefully reach a position that flanked the British line. Leaving behind a strong force of men to line the fenced wood line and occupy the enemy's attention, Jesup continued to press farther to the north with the remainder of his troops, looking to entirely outflank the British positions and come at them without warning from the rear. At the same time, the relocation of Towson's artillery had put it almost within long-range musketry from the Incorporated Militia, whose commander, Lieutenant Colonel Robinson, seeing the enemy artillery as a tempting target of opportunity, ordered the Incorporated Militia to advance and then engage the U.S. guns by wheeling the line forward, like a door swinging on its hinges, with the right-hand end of the line acting as the pivot flank.

As they did so, they came within range and were fired on by the detached troops from Jesup's Twenty-Fifth Regiment and at least one of the guns in Towson's battery. Reacting to this new danger on two flanks, the Incorporated Militia halted its advance and retraced its steps to its original position, whereupon it took up an alignment that would allow it to concentrate its fire upon the increasing numbers of enemy infantry firing from the cover of the woods. For the next half-hour or more, the contest between the Incorporated Militia and Twenty-Fifth became intense, as both sides sought to speed up their reloading and fire as rapidly as possible. According to Lieutenant Duncan Clark of the 7th Company of Incorporated Militia:

> The attack commenced on the left of the British position about 6 o'clock in the afternoon by riflemen from the opposite wood, which was returned by the Incorporated Militia under Lieutenant Colonel Robinson "and by whom" says General Drummond in his official despatch "the brunt of the action was for a considerable time sustained and whose loss has been severe." At this time Ensign

Campbell and two Sergeants were killed, Lieutenant Colonel Robinson and Lieutenant Hamilton were wounded, and Captain MacDonell and Lieutenant Clark at close quarters received balls, one through the sash and the other in the cap without further damage …[1]

Ensign Kilborn of the 10th Company stated:

> As soon as they [the enemy infantry] came in range, although behind a rail fence, along the edge of the woods, we opened fire on them, our men standing exposed in the open field until the approaching darkness and smoke hid them from view, except what could be seen by the fire from their muskets. In this position our men falling fast around us, we stood until some time after darkness had come on; how it was on our right I could not see. Our artillery in the centre kept up a continued roar, nearly drowning the sound of musketry except at short intervals …[2]

By now, the companies of the Incorporated Militia were beginning to run low on ammunition. In response, the wagon containing the regiment's

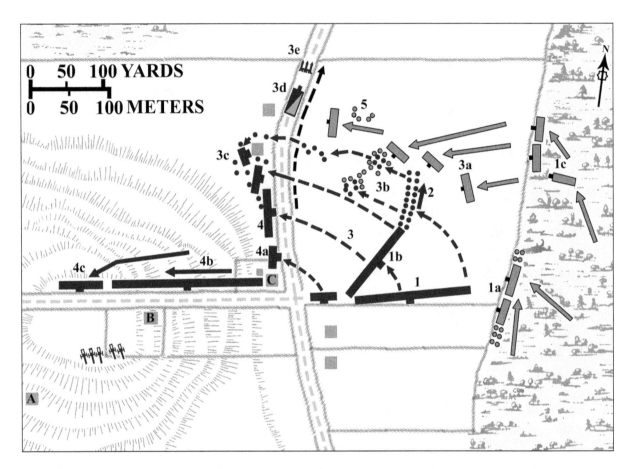

THE BRITISH LEFT FLANK IS TURNED (CIRCA 7:30–9:00 P.M.)

A. Buchner house
B. Lundy's Lane churchyard
C. Johnson's Tavern

1. The Incorporated Militia (IMUC) (1) coming under additional flanking fire from reinforced elements of the Twenty-Fifth Regiment (1a), makes a partial wheel backward on its right to establish a new line (1b) and re-engages, eventually reaching the point of running low on ammunition. As darkness descends, the remaining companies of the Twenty-Fifth Regiment (1c) arrive at the wood line,

outflanking the IMUC and threatening to pass behind the British line to attack it from the rear.

2. Responding to the new threat, the IMUC extends its companies on its left flank into a light infantry formation (2).

3. The IMUC begins to make another backward wheel in its right (3). As it does so, the Twenty-Fifth Regiment charges (3a), capturing men from those companies stationed on the left flank (3b). This attack disrupts the left of the IMUC line, forcing it to regroup once it reaches the Portage Road (3c). Responding to this American flanking threat, the British cavalry detachments (3d) and Congreve rocket detachment (3e) have previously retired north along the Portage Road and effectively leave the action.

4. The companies stationed on the right flank of the Incorporated Militia's line (4), plus the detachment of the 8th (King's) Regiment(4a), having wheeled back in good order, re-form on the west side of the Portage Road, fronting to the east. This frees the 89th Regiment (4b) to move farther to the right (west), while the detachment of the 41st (4c) moves across the hilltop to cover the open right flank of the British line.

5. Elements of the Twenty-Fifth (5) advance to the line of the Portage Road and succeed in capturing additional British troops, including a wounded General Riall and a number of staff riders.

(*N.B.* By this point, darkness has fallen and, compounded by the smoke of weapons firing — the fog of war — all further movements and deployments are done with little or no visibility beyond a few yards.)

reserve cartridges was brought up from the rear to provide ammunition to the men of the line. In addition, officers stationed on the left flank noted a new threat: "Before [it became] too dark, our line had advanced near the woods in front, and I could frequently see the enemy moving to the[ir] right, apparently for the purpose of outflanking us and getting to our rear — nor was I mistaken ..."[3]

Under normal circumstances, this American threat to the regiment's front and flank would have been dealt with by detaching companies to infiltrate the woods and take on the enemy at closer range, sweeping them out and securing that flank. However, placed as it was at the far end of the British line — with no additional support or reinforcements; its commanding officer, Lieutenant Colonel Robinson, incapacitated by a wound that had thrown him from his horse; and its second-in-command, Major Kerby, absent in his duty to locate Hercules Scott's column — it was up to the individual company captains to solve their predicament.

Recognizing that any detachment of manpower would open up an exploitable gap in the British line, the decision was made to have the companies on the right of the regiment remain in line, while the companies on the left would extend their ranks and take up a "light" infantry formation. Seeing his regiment suffering casualties all along its line,

Lieutenant Colonel Robinson was still able to give his men some sagacious advice:

> When his men were acting as Light Infantry, he was knocked off his horse by a ball which struck him in the forehead and came out over his ear. This would have knocked the life out of most men, but it did not knock the wit out of Billy. He was raised and placed in a blanket, his eyes still fixed on his men, who he saw were pushing on in a way to expose themselves. "Stop till I spake to the boys," said he to the men who were carrying him off the field; "Boys!" shouted he, "I have only one remark to make, and that is, that a stump or a log will stand a leaden bullet better than the best of yees, and therefore give them the honour to be your front rank men ..."[4]

He also attempted to extract the regiment from its now dangerously exposed position by ordering it to retire by companies back toward the hill.

Obeying Lieutenant Colonel Robinson's order to retire, the companies on the right-hand end of the line began to fall back in good order. However, in the darkness, those farther to the left were less prompt:

> Sometime after dark, Lieutenant McDougall [6th Company] ... came to me [Ensign Kilborn, 10th Company] saying that I was too far in advance, that our men on the right had fallen back some distance and were likely to fire into us from behind. I told him what I suspected, that they [the enemy] were trying to outflank us and get in our rear. He at once proposed to extend our line towards the river, and at the same time, falling back to regain our line on the right ...[5]

As they did so, Jesup's main force from the Twenty-Fifth Regiment completed its infiltration, charged from the wood, and poured a particularly heavy fire into the rear of the left flank of the Incorporated Militia. Caught between two sets of fire, the men on the left flank recoiled but did not break. Instead, acting upon Lieutenant Colonel Robinson's last active commands on the field, they continued to wheel their line backward ninety degrees. Despite having performed this move during the course of their training at York, it still remained one of the more difficult changes of position that any regiment could be called upon to execute. Now it had to be done in the dark, in the heat of battle, and while under fire from two directions.

For the most part, the companies on the right of the Incorporated Militia's regimental line completed the change with only minor disruptions, but the companies in the centre and left were not as fortunate, and a number of men were cut off and captured:

The wood between the British left and the river was swarming with American riflemen through which a strong division passed imperceived, and about sunset appeared on the Queenston Road in the rear of the British left. Being thus placed between two foes, the Incorporated Militia, under a heavy fire, retired by companies to the hill ...

— Lieutenant Duncan Clark, No. 7 Coy.[6]

Sharp firing, hot work, The In'd M were on the left of Lundy's Lane blasing away like the devil, when a d—d scouting party of the enemy came in our rear and made prisoners of a number of us ... cannot tell what happ'd after being taken prisoner ...

— Ensign Warffe, No. 6 Coy.[7]

While [retiring in the darkness] ... I came directly on a company of Americans formed two deep, the front rank with bayonets charged and the rear rank arms presented ready to fire. I was within twenty feet of them when discovered. The officer at the head of the company demanded a surrender. I hesitated for a short time, but seeing no possibility of escape, I told the men near me to throw down their muskets. Three or four others that were much farther from them than we were attempted to escape, also Lieutenant McDougall. They were shot down and probably killed, except Lieutenant McDougall, who was reported in the General's order of the next day as being mortally wounded with six buckshot. He recovered, however and lived many years after ...

— Ensign Kilborn, No. 10 Coy.[8]

Reaching the west side of the Portage Road, the surviving companies of Incorporated Militia reformed their line at a right angle to the main British position, standing behind the slight cover of a line of split-rail fencing. From here, they began once again to pour out volleys of fire into the approaching enemy, bringing them to a halt. After a short exchange of fire, the Americans began to retire into the darkness of the night, leaving the Incorporated Militia to assess the damage to its ranks, but having successfully secured the flank and rear of the main British line from further attack.

In reviewing this movement, it stands as a credit to the training of Lieutenant Colonel Robinson, and to the relatively short time that it had taken the officers and men of this Canadian regiment to learn their catechism of regular British army drill techniques and battalion field manoeuvres before being thrust into battle (a total of only four months from the time of their amalgamation as a single regimental force (for details see *The Tide of War* from this series and *Redcoated Ploughboys*, both by this author). This successful manoeuvre by the Incorporated Militia also prevented the entire British line from being "rolled up" and almost certainly saved General Drummond from suffering a defeat similar to that of General Riall.

The British line now faced in two directions, with the Incorporated Militia and 8th (King's) Regiment forming a "corner." However, this left the crossroads of Lundy's Lane and the Queenston Road directly in front of the British positions. Fortunately, during the above redeployment and retreat of the left flank, the Congreve rocket troop of the Royal Marines and detachment of 19th Light Dragoons had made the decision to avoid possible capture by retiring from their now exposed position. As a result, they had already moved off north along the Portage Road: and as they are not mentioned in

THE BRITISH LINE REDEPLOYS AND RECEIVES REINFORCEMENTS (CIRCA 9:00–9:45 P.M.)

A. Buchner house
B. Lundy's Lane churchyard
C. Johnson's Tavern
D. Pier's farmstead

1. Major Jesup (Twenty-Fifth) (1) detaches a party of troops to escort his prisoners to the rear (1a) while the remainder of the regiment initially remains adjacent to the Portage Road. He then receives word of a British force to the north on the Portage Road (possibly the 19th Light Dragoons and Congreve rocket detachment). As a result, he withdraws his regiment east (1b) to the wood line and then retires (south). At the main First Brigade position, the Eleventh (1c) and then the Twenty-Second Regiments (1d), having exhausted their ammunition, retire a short distance, leaving only the Ninth and regrouped detachments (1e) still engaging the enemy.

2. In the aftermath of the withdrawal of the Twenty-Fifth's flanking attack, General Drummond reorganizes his line on the hilltop. Most of the companies from the IMUC (2) are moved right (south) to secure the crossroads at right angles to the remainder of the British line. Two companies are detached (2a) and transferred to the right flank to support the 41st Detachment (2b). The 89th Regiment (2c) and 8th (King's) Detachment (2d) both move right (west), to better secure the line of Lundy's Lane and the hilltop.

3. General Drummond orders the recall of the British right flank. In response, the GLI (3) and embodied militias (3a) withdraw northwest toward Lundy's Lane. Norton's advanced band of Native warriors (3b) withdraw toward their main body of Natives

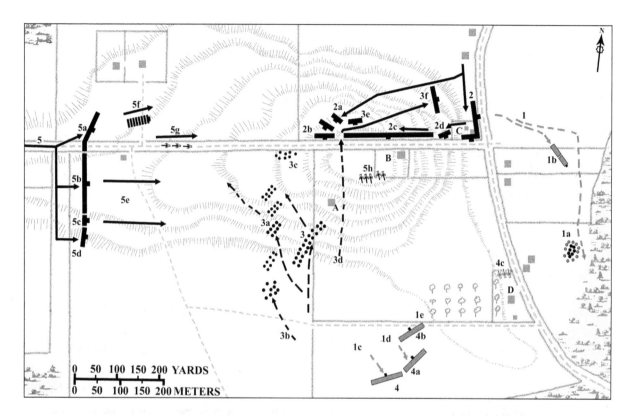

(3c) located on the hill. The three-company detachment of the 1st (Royal Scots) (3d) withdraws north to behind the main British line and re-forms into line (3e) as a reserve before being ordered to move two of its three companies across the hill to support the British left flank (3f).

4. With the British withdrawing, the American First Brigade — Eleventh (4), Twenty-Second (4a), Ninth, and re-formed detachments (4b) — begin the process of re-forming their shattered companies. Towson's artillery (4c) remains at the Pier farmstead (D).

5. The British reinforcement column (5) commanded by Colonel Hercules Scott and guided by Major Kerby (IMUC) arrives on the battlefield from the west. The leading elements of the column's regiments — right flank 103rd (5a), 1st (Royal Scots) (5b), the grenadier company of the 103rd (5c), and flank companies of the 104th (5d) — form line across and to the south of Lundy's Lane before advancing (5e). The left flank of the 103rd Regiment (5f) advances separately toward the north side of the hill, while three artillery pieces (5g) move directly up Lundy's Lane toward the established battery on the hilltop (5h).

any other accounts detailing the events of the night, can for all intents and purposes be considered to have played no further active part in the battle. This redeployment also left Jesup's American troops controlling the open ground between the woods and the east side of the Queenston/Portage Road above (north of) Lundy's Lane, threatening to cut off any further British reinforcements from the north and intercepting anyone who attempted to use the road to move toward Queenston. In this way, a number of officers and men, including a wounded General Riall, fell into the hands of the Americans.

With daylight gone, his ammunition depleted, and encumbered with a large body of prisoners, Jesup received word that General Drummond was moving up the road from Queenston with a large body of reinforcements (leading to the conclusion that at least some of the American officers were still not aware that Drummond was already present with the army on the hilltop) and that Scott's main body had met with a severe mauling on the far side of the hill.

Assessing his position as being more than a little exposed and concerned at being cut off himself, Jesup ordered his remaining troops to break off and retire to Wilson's Tavern with their haul of prisoners. This American retreat temporarily ended the threat to the British left flank but saw a number of men taken into captivity:

After I had, with five or six men, surrendered, the Lieutenant in command of the company of about sixty men, formed his men in a hollow square, placed his prisoners within it, marched us round near the river and up by the Falls in rear of their army and beyond the reach of a shot from either side, placed me under a strong guard in charge of his junior officer, and with the balance of his company returned back to the battlefield …

— Ensign Kilborn, No. 10 Coy., Incorporated Militia[9]

While Jesup's information about the pending arrival of Drummond was obviously incorrect, and is more likely to have been a misidentification of the retreated rocket battery and light dragoons, his information about the fate of Scott's brigade on the far side of the hill was certainly no exaggeration. There, having already suffered significant casualties at its initial stationary position, the First Brigade's subsequent advance only served to increase its rate of attrition as the range steadily decreased.

Responding to this American movement, General Drummond countered by ordering three companies of the 1st (Royal Scots) Regiment (Captain Brereton) to move down from the crest of the hill to fire upon the advancing enemy from the front. At the same time, detachments from the Glengarry Light Infantry (Lieutenant Colonel Battersby), the 2nd York Embodied Militia (Major Simons), and Natives (Captain Norton), far from retiring, swung even farther forward in an arc and succeeded in outflanking the Americans. As a result, the combined fire of these units brought the American First Brigade to a complete halt and a firefight of volleys ensued between the opposing lines. At the same time, the British artillery on the hilltop continued to pound the exposed Americans at an even better and more deadly range than before. Caught in this crossfire, Scott's already depleted brigade was being torn to shreds. Desperate to contain the Canadian and Native outflanking movement, the left-hand part of the Eleventh Regiment successfully wheeled back, in a mirror image of what had been done on the far side of the battlefield by the Incorporated Militia, while the Ninth and the re-formed and returned detachments of men who had earlier routed wheeled forward to the left. However, by this point the earlier expenditure of firing had depleted much of the line's immediate ammunition and was becoming a serious issue. As Sergeant Blake of the Eleventh Regiment later recorded:

[After] the 11th regiment broke and retired through the woods, I got a few men collected ... we then marched into the road; we stopped there for a short time; we then marched into a field the other side of the road and remained there for a short time ... we were on the move to return back into the road, when an officer rode up and ordered us to the field of action; we then proceeded and formed on the right of the first brigade; we opened fire upon the enemy; the remainder of the brigade were out of cartridges ...[10]

— Sergeant Blake,
Eleventh Regiment

Inevitably, the casualties being inflicted on the American First Brigade brought it to the point where even its most aggressive officers began to recommend an immediate withdrawal under the cover of the battlefield smoke and the darkness that had now covered the entire ground. In addition, as mentioned above, many soldiers were running out of ammunition and when no resupply was forthcoming, company after company fell silent, leaving the men exposed to the enemy's musket and cannon fire and with only Blake's latecomers still firing.

The opportunity was now there for General Drummond to press forward and sweep the remnants of the First Brigade from the field, but with the onset of darkness and the dense smoke produced by the continual firing of the weapons, visibility had been reduced to a matter of a few yards. Certain that additional American support was immediately behind Scott's depleted line, and unable to see anything of the American strengths or dispositions, Drummond chose instead to remain on the defensive. To this end he ordered the recall of his advanced regiments on the right flank and redeployed his available forces across the hilltop. To supplement this line he also detached a number of companies from the Incorporated Militia to fill gaps at the left, centre, and right of his new line. Shortly thereafter, upon the return of the 1st (Royal Scots), Drummond initially established them behind the line as a reserve, but then detached one company to remain while the remainder were moved over to the British left to cover that flank and support the remaining companies of the Incorporated Militia.

Fortunately for General Drummond, Major Kerby succeeded in locating Colonel Hercules Scott's column and successfully guided it to the battlefield. Marching up Lundy's Lane from the west, and despite having just made a forced march of nearly twenty miles (32 kilometers), the first of these exhausted and straggling units (the 103rd and 104th Regiments) were immediately pressed into combat, creating an entirely new British line running north–south. Unfortunately, due to the darkness, no proper assessment of the relative placements or strengths of the formations already engaged could be determined, beyond that provided by the sounds of reverberating gunfire and the sight of brief flashes of flame coming from across the open fields. As a result, only the left wing of the 103rd Regiment and the three 6-pounder guns of the artillery were moved toward the hill. Major Kerby, having now completed his assigned duty, left the column to rejoin his regiment, only to discover upon his arrival on the other side of the hill that with the loss of Lieutenant Colonel Robinson, he was now in charge of the regiment.

CHAPTER 6

The Guns Must Be Taken!

Previously, back at Chippawa, and as the shadows of the day had lengthened, General Brown had heard the sounds of heavy gunfire coming from the north. Upon receiving Scott's initial report, he ordered General Ripley to advance his Second Brigade. At the same time, General Porter was directed to assemble his depleted militia force (detachments having previously been sent to Fort Erie, Lewiston, Buffalo, and Fort Schlosser) on the north bank of the Chippawa and await further orders.

Collecting the Twenty-First Regiment (Colonel Miller), the Twenty-Third Regiment (Major McFarland), as well as two artillery batteries (Captain Biddle's and Captain Richie's), which were already in the process of assembling for their evening parade, Brigadier General Ripley began an immediate and rapid advance toward Lundy's Lane. This force was then joined by Lieutenant Riddle's detachment of the Nineteenth Regiment, which arrived back from its reconnaissance and, without making any report, simply joined the column and marched back to the battlefield. Shortly after, the Second Brigade was followed by three companies of the First Regiment (Lieutenant Colonel Nicholas). This unit had just arrived on the Niagara frontier that morning, was still in the process of rowing over troops from the American side of the river, and without orders had followed the old military maxim of marching to the sound of the guns. While marching toward Lundy's Lane, Brown received a further report from Scott through Major Wood (Corps of Engineers), calling for reinforcements. In response, Brown sent back orders to General Porter to bring forward his

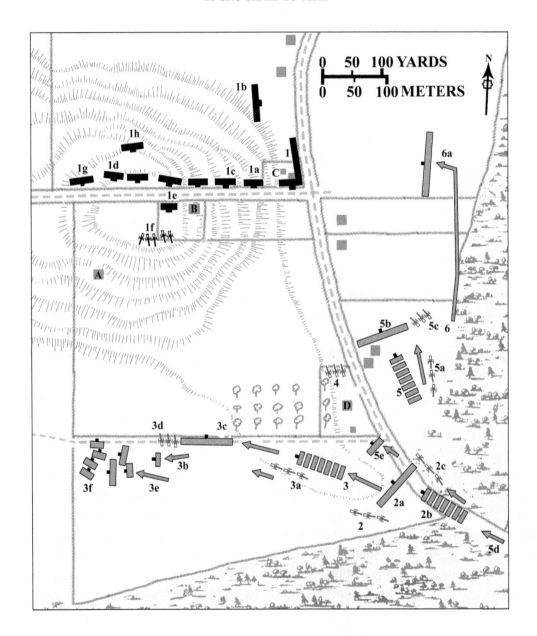

THE AMERICAN SECOND BRIGADE ARRIVES AND DEPLOYS (CIRCA 9:00–9:45 P.M.)

A. Buchner house
B. Lundy's Lane churchyard
C. Johnson's Tavern
D. Pier's farmstead

1. The IMUC (1) secure the crossroads, supported on their right by the detachment of the 8th (King's) (1a) and on their left rear by two companies of the 1st (Royal Scots) (1b). On the hilltop, companies of the main body of the 89th (1c–1d) are dispersed to cover more ground, while a detachment (1e) is moved forward to support the guns (1f). On the far right, a combined detachment of the 41st regiment and two companies of the Incorporated Militia (1g) complete the British front line, with only a single company of the 1st (Royal Scots) (1h) being in reserve.
2. General Brown with General Ripley's Second Brigade enters the field. Because of the darkness and at Brown's orders, they take up an initial position at the edge of the woods (Richie's artillery [2], Twenty-First Regiment [2a], Twenty-Third Regiment [2b], and Biddle's artillery [2c]) until the circumstances prevailing on the battlefield can be determined. In response, the Twenty-First forms line, while the Twenty-Third remains in column, as do the two artillery batteries.
3. Receiving reports of the First Brigade's heavy casualties and difficulties and believing his position is too far back to be effective, Ripley orders his brigade to advance. The Twenty-First Regiment re-forms its column (3) and, accompanied by Richie's artillery battery (3a), move left (west) to bypass the obstruction of Pier's farmstead (D). Passing the farm's orchard, Riddle's detachment of the Nineteenth Regiment (3b) is directed to break off and support Scott's force on the left, while the Twenty-First and artillery advance (north) and form their line-of-battle (3c-3d) on the right of Winfield Scott's severely mauled First Brigade (which by now has marched west [3e] and is attempting to re-form amalgamated companies [3f]).
4. Towson's battery (4) in Pier's farm (D).
5. On the right, the Twenty-Third Regiment (5), accompanied by Biddle's battery (5a), advance and form their line-of-battle on the east of the Portage Road (5b, 5c). At the same time, the detachment of the First Regiment (Lieutenant Colonel Nicholas) arrives on the field (5d), but without having any orders and simply looking to join Ripley's Second Brigade. Receiving information of the brigade's move toward the left flank from an officer in the darkness, Nicholas moves his force down the Portage Road toward the Pier farmstead orchard (5e) in his attempt to find Ripley.
6. The Twenty-Fifth Regiment (6), having deposited its prisoners and having been notified of General Brown's reinforcement by Captain Biddle's artillery unit, re-enters the field and advances in the direction of the crossroads by moving down the eastern line of the open ground (6a).

Third Brigade, as well as any other units that could be formed from those troops still in camp.

Marching north, General Brown and the Second Brigade finally arrived on the battlefield shortly after darkness had fallen, but because of the lack of visibility, Brown had no immediate way of assessing the tactical or strategic situation. As a result, he halted the Second Brigade and ordered it to form a line directly along the wood line, while he moved forward to assess the situation and locate Scott. In fact, only the Twenty-First formed a line, while the Twenty-Third remained in column off to the right.

Hearing of the mauling still being suffered by the First Brigade from some of the returning walking wounded and of the commanding position of the British line on the hilltop, General Ripley made the unilateral decision not to wait for General Brown's return, but to advance his brigade closer to the hill, where its volleys could be more effective on the enemy and simultaneously draw British fire away from the First Brigade. However, to do so by a direct march to the front would mean pushing through the heavily fenced and wooded Pier's farm. Instead, Ripley decided to move by passing on either side of the farm and then form his line-of-battle with Towson's guns at his centre and his own two batteries on the flanks. After re-forming the column of the Twenty-First Regiment, the two infantry regiments moved around to either side of the Pier farmstead and Towson's artillery position, each being accompanied by one of the newly arrived artillery batteries. Once they had passed the farm's obstacle, both regiments and their associated artillery units deployed into line, with the artillery immediately opening fire toward the hilltop and thereby drawing fire back in return. At the

same time, having by now rejoined the Second Brigade, Brown sent his aide, Major William McCree, assisted by Lieutenant David Douglass, to secretly reconnoitre the British positions, as it was obvious that the primary threat of the British guns had to be eliminated as soon as possible.

On the crest of the hill, the previous accuracy and effectiveness of the British artillery had steadily been degraded by the onset of darkness, and any firing done from this point was to be random at best. Furthermore, the relentless firing had depleted the available musket ammunition within the advanced infantry line. As a result, General Drummond was forced to strip those units of the embodied militias being held in reserve on the British right of their ammunition, thus effectively rendering them useless for further participation in the battle. However, it is known that many of these men subsequently braved the thickest parts of the battlefield fighting in order to act as field couriers, relaying messages and resupplying ammunition, or acting as field medics by assisting the wounded to the rear for treatment.

At this point in the story, it is perhaps worth pausing to understand that due to the onset of darkness reducing visibility and the fact that the two sides worked on entirely independent time settings (there being no such thing as a standardized time zone), subsequent "eyewitness" accounts of the battle list sequences of events or timings that are disjointed and sometimes entirely contradictory, especially when comparing American and British/Canadian versions of the battle. Consequently, compiling a coherent version of events becomes more and more difficult to achieve as the battle progresses. The following is the author's interpretation of events, which may not necessarily coincide with other authors' accounts.

Meanwhile, back on the hilltop, although he had previously recalled his right wing, General Drummond appears to have failed to notify the newly arriving regiments of the expected return of the friendly troops to their front. As a result, in the darkness, the 103rd and 104th Regiments mistook the retiring formations of Glengarry Light Infantry and embodied militias for Americans making an attack. Consequently, the two regiments opened fire on their hapless comrades, causing casualties and routing the returning units, who scattered to the left and right before passing through or around the newly arrived British line, thereby also disrupting and delaying its commitment to the battle.

Once they had passed behind the British western lines, the officers and NCOs of the Glengarries and militias had to begin the difficult task of locating and re-forming their companies in the dark. At the same time, Norton's advanced Native party, retiring toward their fellow warriors on the hill, found upon their arrival that the men had disappeared (most likely having joined in the precipitant retreat on that flank). Standing alone in the middle of a dark battlefield and not knowing where their comrades had gone, at least some of the party and Norton himself must have decided to go where they knew their presence would be supported by friendly troops, for shortly thereafter, Norton's own account of the battle places him directly behind the main battery of British guns.

Unaware of this series of events on his flank, General Drummond concentrated on what he believed to be the main threat to his position; namely, the flashes of gunfire directly to his front. Unfortunately, while he correctly assessed the direction of this threat, General Drummond then failed to establish a protective advanced covering screen of light troops on the slope below his battery of guns, despite the fact that virtually half his force was trained for exactly that purpose. Instead, the main British line-of-battle was drawn up some way behind the guns, on the north side of Lundy's Lane, while only a small detachment of the 89th Regiment was placed on the south side of the road and in immediate proximity to the guns. Consequently, the centre of the British position and the vital guns were effectively left exposed to attack. As a result, General Brown soon learned from his reconnaissance that the way forward was

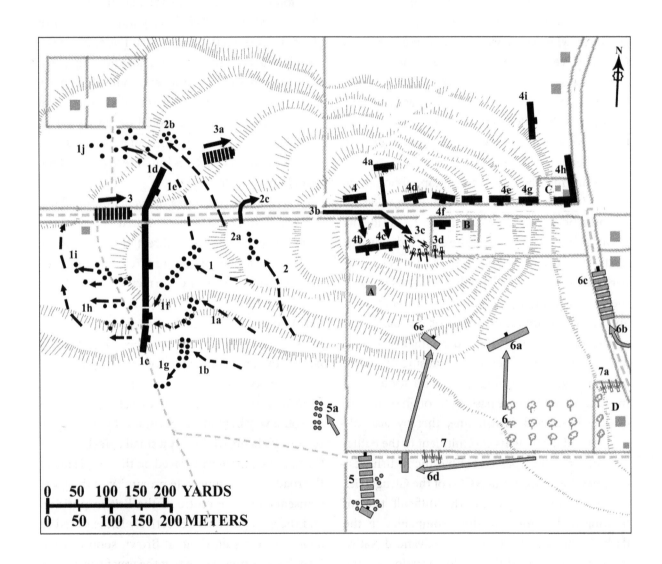

FRIENDLY FIRE DISRUPTS THE BRITISH RIGHT FLANK AND THE AMERICAN ATTACK ON THE HILL BEGINS (CIRCA 9:30–9:50 P.M.)

A. Buchner house
B. Lundy's Lane churchyard
C. Johnson's Tavern
D. Pier's farmstead

1. Because of the complete darkness, on the far west of the field, the retiring units, GLI (1), and embodied militias (1a, 1b) are mistakenly fired on by Hercules Scott's line (1c–1d) and suffer casualties. Routed, the disordered units pass through and around Hercules Scott's line (1e, 1f, 1g) before beginning to regroup in the rear (1h, 1i, 1j).
2. The advanced elements of the Native allies (under Norton) (2) reach the location where the remaining Natives were left (2a), only to find they have disappeared (having likely joined in the rout/retreat) (2b). Norton and at least part of his band then move round the hill (2c) toward the last known British positions at the crest.
3. The last unit of Hercules Scott's column, the 8th (King's) Regiment (3), arrives on the field and is placed in reserve. The detached left flank of the 103rd (3a) continues to move toward the north side of the hill, while the column's artillery (3b) arrives at the hilltop and begins to unlimber its guns (3c) prior to adding to the British bombardment from the hilltop battery (3d).
4. Across the hill, the British line stabilizes its position: the combined detachment (det.) of 41st and Incorporated Militia (4) and the single company of the 1st (Royal Scots) (4a) move forward (4b, 4c) to protect the right (west) flank of the battery position. The main companies of the 89th (4d–4e) line the north side of Lundy's Lane, while the advanced company of the 89th (4f) is on the south side.

The det. 8th (King's) (4g) is alongside Johnson's Tavern (C), while the remaining companies of the Incorporated Militia (4h) occupy its grounds at the crossroads, forming a corner. On the east slope of the hill, the remaining two companies of the 1st (Royal Scots) (4i) secure the British left flank.

5. While the remnants of the First Brigade continue to establish a column of amalgamated companies from all three of its regiments (5), Lieutenant Riddle's company is sent forward (5a) to provide picket cover (in case of a return by the British on the western flank).
6. Given the order to attack the British battery position, the Twenty-First Regiment (6) begins its advance in line (6a) only to be temporarily halted by General Drummond until he reverses his decision and the advance continues. The Twenty-Third re-forms its column (6b) and marches directly up the Portage Road (6c) toward the crossroads. The First Regiment's detachment (6d) moves west along the lane running beside Pier's farm until it reaches General Ripley's First Brigade position (5) looking for directions; it then moves northeast toward the hill (6e).
7. Lieutenant Richie's battery (7), Lieutenant Towson's battery (7a).

open for an assault on the guns under the cover of darkness.

On the open ground to the south of the hill, the Second Brigade had maintained its position and drawn fire away from the First Brigade, only to now have this duty countermanded as the order to attack the hilltop arrived. On the left of the Chippawa–Queenston road, the Twenty-First Regiment began to demolish a fence that now blocked their way, while the Twenty-Third re-formed their column. Their joint orders were to attack the battery, with Miller's Twenty-First Regiment moving directly up the slope, while McFarland's Twenty-Third column would advance along the road, under Ripley's personal supervision, before wheeling left into line and assaulting the artillery position from the flank. According to General Ripley's later account:

> I adopted this route upon the circumstances of that regiment [the Twenty-Third] being principally composed of recruits and not having had command of it until four or five days previous to our march from Buffalo, I felt apprehensive that it would fall into confusion from the destructive fire of the enemy, while I felt confident of the extraordinary efforts from the veterans of the 21st Regt ...[1]

At the same time, off to the left of the Second Brigade's position, General Brown and his small headquarters party were riding across the open ground at the foot of the hill, when they realized that a body of British troops was stationed on the hilltop and immediately to the west of the British guns. This consisted of Captain Brereton's company of the 1st (Royal Scots) Regiment, the amalgamated companies from the Incorporated Militia (Captain Fraser, Captain MacDonell), and the light company of the 41st Regiment (Captain Glew). Concerned that this force could outflank the American assault on the guns, Brown crossed to the American centre and temporarily halted Miller's troops, who were still in the process of demolishing the fence. However, after a few moments' conversation with Colonel Miller, Brown finally committed to the attack, countermanding himself and redirecting the Twenty-First to storm the guns. He then continued east until he reached the Portage Road, looking for the Twenty-Third Regiment in order to bring it forward as well.

Meanwhile, as they advanced up the slope under cover of the darkness, Miller's Twenty-First Regiment heard firing coming from both the right and left of their position.

The noise from the right was caused by the Twenty-Third Regiment, which had run into a wall of fire from the British "corner," formed by the remainder of the companies of the Incorporated Militia occupying the grounds of the Forsyth Tavern. This fire had quickly routed the Twenty-Third, killing Major McFarland and most of the leading company in that column. According to General Ripley:

The 23rd marched in column …. At this moment, a detachment farther down Lundy's road in front opened a fire upon them. With one accord the column fired without orders, immediately broke and sought refuge behind a house …[2]

The firing from the Twenty-First's left, on the other hand, was the result of the unannounced and unexpected arrival of a large detachment of the First Regiment, under Lieutenant Colonel Nicholas. Although this regiment had only just arrived on the Niagara frontier, was not officially incorporated into the Second Brigade, and had neither orders nor information about what lay ahead, it had nevertheless marched to the sound of the guns and entered the field of battle, only to immediately come under fire from the British guns on the hilltop, which were firing blindly into the darkness in hopes of hitting formations using the main Portage Road.

Receiving only a general set of directions from a passing officer that suggested the Second Brigade had moved off to the left (west) of his present position, Lieutenant Colonel Nicholas feared that if he advanced directly toward the hill in the darkness he could inadvertently fire on his own side. He therefore marched his detachment diagonally (northwest) across the field in pursuit of General Ripley. Instead he arrived at the position of the First Brigade whilst General Scott was in the process of re-forming a single column of eight platoons or companies of men from the remnants of the three regiments that had only a short time before called themselves the First Brigade. Unable to elicit any additional concrete information of where the Second Brigade was stationed, beyond that it was somewhere forward and to the right of his current location, Nicholas's small force then moved back diagonally (northeast) across the field. However, when they were still unable to locate Ripley's brigade, they simply headed toward the hilltop.

This advance continued until Nicholas suddenly realized he was almost on top of the British lines, as he came under fire from the British battery and a body of troops stationed to the west of the guns. These troops were the aforementioned detachments of the 1st (Royal Scots), 41st Regiment and Incorporated Militia, who had detected Nicholas's approach and opened fire, thus alerting Miller of activities occurring to the west of his advance. After exchanging fire with the British, Nicholas knew that any further advance would be suicidal, whereupon he ordered his force to "Right About Face."[3] Leading his men back down the slope, Nicholas moved his small force to his left (west), where it found some degree of cover behind a white farmhouse (the Buchner farmhouse), situated on the lower slopes of the southwest side of the hill.

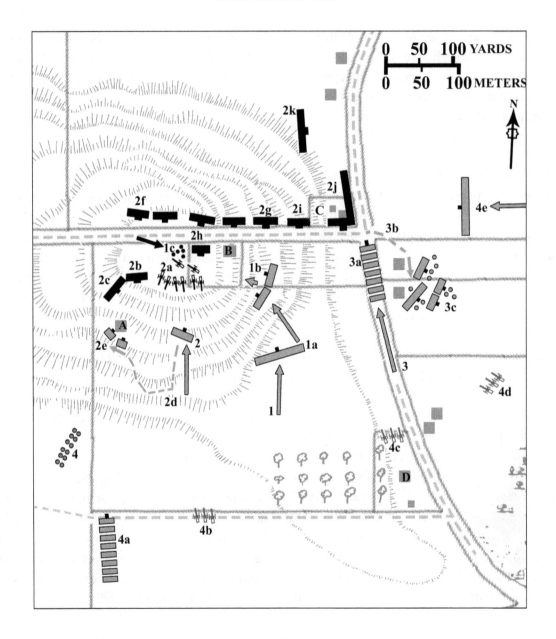

THE AMERICAN ATTACK APPROACHES THE HILL (CIRCA 9:50 P.M.)

A. Buchner house
B. Lundy's Lane churchyard
C. Johnson's Tavern
D. Pier's farmstead

(*N.B.* The following events happen almost at the same time and in the dark.)

1. Undetected, the Twenty-First Regiment (1) marches up through the centre-east side of the hill (1a) until it reaches the overgrown fences that mark the east and south boundaries of the hill-top cemetery (B). It then lines the fences (1b) as Norton's Natives (1c) arrive from the west.

2. On the centre-west side of the hill, the advancing detachment from the First Regiment (2) comes under fire from the British artillery (2a) on the crest, supported by the company of 1st (Royal Scots) (2b), 41st, and Incorporated Militia (2c). Under this combined fire, the First Regiment retreats downhill (2d), before moving across and behind the Buchner farm buildings (A), where they begin to re-form (2e). The remainder of the British line remains as before: main companies of the 89th (2f–2g); the advanced company of the 89th (2h) det. 8th (King's) (2i); companies of the Incorporated Militia (2j); and companies of the 1st (Royal Scots) (2k).

3. At the bottom of the slope on the east side of the hill, the Twenty-Third Regiment (3) marches up the Portage Road and almost reaches the crossroads (3a) with Lundy's Lane, when it comes under heavy point-blank fire from the Incorporated Militia (2j), who have just been rejoined by Major Kerby at the grounds of Johnson's Tavern (C). After having the head of its column wiped out, the remainder of the Twenty-Third's column fires a disorganized volley and routs (3b). Retreating in disorder, the Twenty-Third is eventually halted behind some nearby farm buildings, where it begins to re-form (3c).

4. Around the foot of the hill, the remaining American units act independent of the action at the hill. Lieutenant Riddle's company (4) remains as pickets. General Scott's remnant brigade (4a) completes its unification of all surviving troops into a single composite column. Richie's battery (4b), Towson's battery (4c), and Biddle's battery (4d) presumably cease firing to avoid inflicting casualties on their own troops engaged in the attack and may have limbered their guns. Major Jesup's Twenty-Fifth Regiment (4e) advances toward the crossroads from the east.

These two separate and uncoordinated movements, while achieving little beyond mounting the American casualty roll, did distract the British gunners on the hilltop, as well as the troops on either side. As a result, Miller's troops were able to creep up through the undefended centre to within point-blank range of the guns. There they formed a line behind the cover of some low bushes and a split-rail fence that ran around the perimeter of the churchyard. As they prepared to fire, they were finally spotted by the small party of Natives under Norton. But before the Natives could raise the alarm, Miller's troops delivered a devastating volley into the unprepared battery at almost point-blank

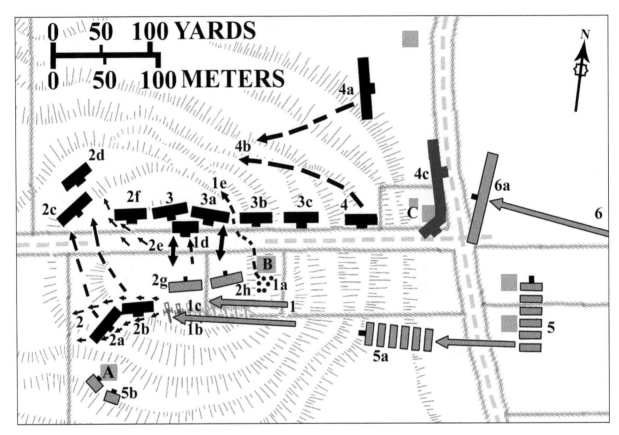

THE AMERICANS CAPTURE THE BRITISH ARTILLERY AND FIGHT OFF THE INITIAL LIMITED BRITISH COUNTERATTACK, WHILE FIGHTING RENEWS AT THE CROSSROADS (CIRCA 9:55–10:15 P.M.)

A. Buchner house
B. Lundy's Lane churchyard
C. Johnson's Tavern

1. With Miller's Twenty-First Regiment (1) in position along the overgrown fences bordering the Lundy's Lane hilltop churchyard and cemetery (B), they are detected at the last minute by some of John Norton's Native band (1a), just as the Americans fire and charge (1b), overrunning the British artillery position (1c) on the hilltop and driving off the advanced detachment (det.) of the 89th Regiment (1d) and Norton's Native band (1e).

2. The American attack causes the surviving British

artillery horses from the newly arrived guns to stampede (2) through the units stationed on the right of the guns— combined 41st/ IMUC (2a) and det.1st (Royal Scots) (2b) — forcing these units to withdraw in order to reorganize (2c, 2d). The artillery horses of the already-established guns, stationed to the rear of the battery (2e), similarly disrupt the right flank of the 89th (2f). Securing the position, the Americans imprison the surviving gun crews in the church building (B) and begin to form a line-of-battle immediately behind (north of) the guns (2g–2h).

3. With the British right flank disrupted and partially retired (2c, 2d), the initial counterattack is made by the central group of companies of the 89th Regiment (1d, 3–3a), but is driven off. The remaining companies of the 89th (3b, 3c) retain their positions.

4. While the main British line regroups, the detachment of the 8th (King's) Regiment (4) and the main detachment of the 1st (Royal Scots) (4a) are withdrawn from the left flank (4b) to support the British counterattack against the hilltop, leaving the reduced companies of Incorporated Militia (4c) alone at the crossroads.

5. Under orders from General Brown, the re-formed Twenty-Third Regiment (5) moves across to the left (west) and begins its march to join the Twenty-First on the hilltop (5a). The detachment of the First Regiment (5b) remains behind the Buchner farmstead building (A).

6. The Twenty-Fifth Regiment (6) arrives at the crossroads (6a) and, being detected, is fired on by the Incorporated Militia (4c). The two regiments then engage in heavy close-quarter volley action across the width of the road.

range. Most of the artillerymen serving the guns were thus either killed or wounded by this single volley, while the teams of horses that had just been brought up with the additional guns were similarly killed or stampeded through the line of the troops to the right (west) of the guns, which in turn disordered their formation and prevented them from mounting a counterattack until they had fallen back and re-formed. Similarly, the horses from the artillery units stationed behind the guns on the hilltop since the start of the engagement also bolted to their rear, impacting on the right flank companies of the 89th Regiment. Following up upon their lethal fire, the Twenty-First Regiment charged forward with the bayonet, overrunning the guns and throwing the single advanced company of the 89th

The Battle of Bridgewater. W. Strickland, artist and engraver, not dated. A post-war impression of the height of the battle of Lundy's Lane, or Bridgewater as early American accounts named it. While inaccurate in details, it is evocative of the atmosphere of the conflict.

Regiment back toward their own main line, capturing in the process a combined total of around forty artillery and infantrymen, who were quickly secured inside the adjacent church building.

Within the main British line, located farther back from the artillery position on the crest, the detachments of the 89th Regiment were caught off guard by the sudden volley and charge of the Americans.

This was then compounded by the stampede of the artillery horses through their right-hand units. Fortunately, General Drummond was nearby and ordered the 89th to make an immediate counterattack to regain the vital position. Marching forward, those companies immediately to the rear of the guns, and not otherwise disordered by the stampede, opened fire into the milling mass of dark shapes vaguely discernible amongst the cannon. Attempting to continue with the bayonet, they

THE BRITISH MAKE TWO ADDITIONAL LIMITED COUNTERATTACKS TO REGAIN THE HILL AND THE AMERICAN LINE IS REINFORCED (CIRCA 10:15–10:30 P.M.)

A. Buchner house
B. Lundy's Lane churchyard
C. Johnson's Tavern

1. Following reinforcement, the British line — amalgamated IMUC / 41st Regiment (1); reunified companies of the 1st Royal Scots (1a); the 89th (1b); and det. 8th (King's) (1c) — makes two additional counterattacks upon the Twenty-First Regiment (1d) but is unable to break the American position and eventually retires toward the northwest side of the hill (1e, 1f).
2. The Twenty-Third (2) arrives at the hilltop in column, and is formed into line (2a) to the right of the Twenty-First (1d), just as the British are retiring.
3. At the crossroads, the Twenty-Fifth Regiment (3) continues exchanging fire with the Incorporated Militia (3a) at around the time the renewed British

counterattacks are taking place. In response to the sounds of fighting in the darkness coming from their rear and the perceived threat of being attacked from both the front and rear, the Incorporated Militia withdraws to the northeast side of the hill, where they initially establish a new position to cover that flank (3b). Following the failure of the initial counterattacks, they are ordered west to join in the preparations for the main British counterattack on the hill (3c).

4. Before it can advance, the Twenty-Fifth (3) is ordered by General Brown to disengage (4) and abandon its flanking movement, and instead to march to the hilltop from the southeast (4a).
5. The re-formed detachment from the First Regiment (5) moves out from behind the Buchner house (A) and marches up to the hilltop, passing the captured British battery (5a). Upon arriving, the Twenty-Fifth initially forms behind the right flank of the American line (5b), but is then repositioned by Miller to the left flank (5c) in order to extend his line to the west. With both armies temporarily disengaged, the fighting lulls and both sides redeploy their forces

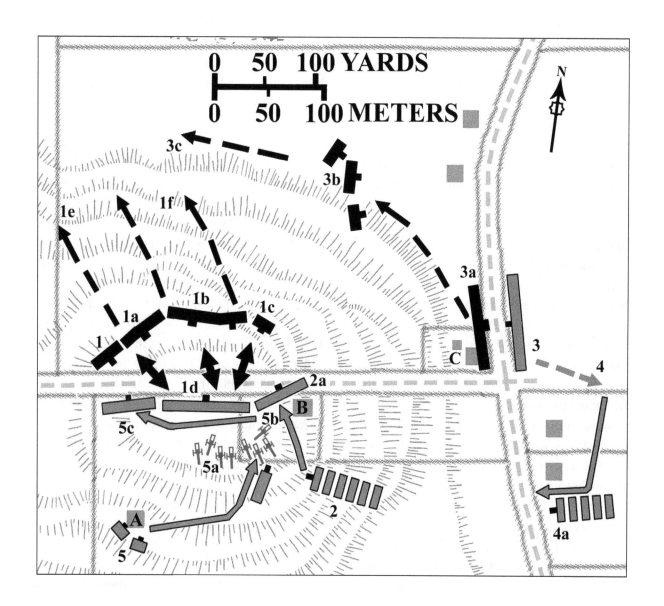

were met with fire from the re-forming Americans, which halted the British advance. As a result, the conflict bogged down into a stationary firefight, at a range so close that the long flashes of flame from the muzzles of the muskets virtually overlapped each other and the sonic concussion of each firing physically battered the soldiers being targeted. Furthermore, the musket balls did double damage, as the deadly force of the point-blank firing occasionally propelled the balls completely through the bodies of the front rank and into the men standing in the rear line.

Unable to dislodge the Americans, the 89th companies were eventually forced to retreat, but soon returned with reinforcements that included additional companies of the 89th and the now re-formed detachments of Incorporated Militia, the 41st, and the 1st (Royal Scots) detachment. Twice more, the two lines clashed and the carnage continued, including the wounding of General Drummond, who was hit in the neck by a musket ball that only narrowly missed the commander's main artery. But the Twenty-First Regiment held to its advantage of the higher ground, eventually forcing the British to withdraw into the darkness, leaving their entire artillery park in American hands.

During this same period, and just after leaving Miller's force, General Brown had also heard the sound of firing from the supposed position of the Twenty-Third Regiment. Hastening forward, Brown met his aides, Captain Spencer (Twenty-Ninth Regiment) and Major Wood (U.S. Engineers), who had been undertaking detached duties for the general in the confusion of the darkness. Together the three rode east until they reached the Portage Road and then turned left (north), heading toward the junction with Lundy's Lane. As a result, they were in the process of passing behind the re-forming lines of the Twenty-Third, when the noise of firing from the dark hilltop announced Miller's attack had begun. Noting that there were no answering sounds of artillery fire, General Brown concluded that Miller's efforts had been successful. He therefore ordered Ripley to cease his planned flanking attack and instead directed him to move back around to the left and ascend the hill from the south, following Miller's route, in order to support the Twenty-First. Brown and his aides then pressed forward along the road, intending to reconnoitre toward Lundy's Lane. As a result, they nearly ran directly into a fierce firefight that erupted immediately before them when someone in the darkness yelled out "They are the Yankees ..."[4]

This warning call possibly came from Major Kerby, who had located the now isolated companies of the Incorporated Militia still stationed on the northwest side of the road junction and had taken over command of the regiment. However, the cause of the alarm was not Brown's party, but Jesup's Twenty-Fifth Regiment, which had been attempting to place itself on the left rear of the British line once more. According to Brown's eyewitness testimony, "The moment the British officer gave Major Jesup notice of having discovered him, Jesup ordered his command to fire. The lines could not have been more than four rods apart [22 yards, or 20.5 meters]. The slaughter was dreadful …"[5]

Although heavily outnumbered and separated from the remainder of the British line (because the regular troops that had previously been placed on that flank had been withdrawn to bolster the centre of the British position), the Canadian militiamen stood their ground and traded volleys with Jesup's regulars. However, once the renewed sounds of even heavier firing began coming from the hilltop (as the repeated British counterattacks on the guns began), Kerby recognized that his small force was in immediate danger of being surrounded. In response to this threat, Kerby made an orderly fighting retreat by moving his command north, along the west side of Portage Road, in a "leapfrogging" of detachments before swinging them west around the foot of the hill. There he was able to renew his contact with the left of the main British line and take up a new defensive position on the north side of the hill, facing northeast. Apart from this thin screen of men from the Incorporated

Militia, the way forward was now open for Jesup to swing around the east side of the hill and engage the British from the rear. However, prevented by the darkness from knowing what forces lay before him and uncertain how best to proceed, the opportunity passed when General Brown arrived and informed Jesup that his force was required on the hilltop in support of Miller and Ripley. In Jesup's own words, he "abandoned his position, moved back and joined General Ripley on the heights, by whom he was posted with his command on the right of the line which was then forming …"[6]

On top of the hill, the desperate fight to hold on to the guns had cost Miller's command dearly and he urgently needed reinforcements. Fearing another British counterattack would regain the guns, Miller ordered Lieutenant Holding and a party of men from his company to remove the captured artillery pieces in the direction of the American side of the hill. He also sent his aide to seek out reinforcements. Moving down the hill, the aide came across the First Regiment, still sheltering behind the Buchner house. Receiving new directions to move to the hilltop, Lieutenant Colonel Nicholas led his detachment forward and initially began to deploy on the right of the hilltop American position. However, this was quickly countermanded by Miller, who directed the First to move to the other flank, as this was the direction in which the British had retreated. In response, Nicholas led his men behind the American line and took up a position to the left of Miller's Twenty-First Regiment. Shortly thereafter, the Twenty-Third Regiment also arrived and formed line to the right of the Twenty-First, creating a new line of defence that stretched from the churchyard on the east, across the crest of the hill, and toward a line of fencing that at the time marked the western boundary of the Buchner farmstead and today marks the line of Drummond Road.

Arriving on the hilltop, General Ripley now took overall command and, agreeing with Miller's assessment that the main threat to his position would probably come from the American left, he moved his entire line farther in that direction. He also countermanded Miller's removal order for the captured artillery, as he believed these guns could be brought back into action against their former owners. In support of this, he sent word back to the foot of the hill for Colonel Hindman to bring forward the three American artillery batteries. This was done in rapid order, with each unit making its own way forward.

Upon the arrival of the American artillery units, Captain Towson placed his guns on the forward slope of the hill on the north side of Lundy's Lane and to the right of the Twenty-Third Regiment's new position, while Captain Ritchie's battery was located forward of the First Regiment, sweeping

the ground in the direction the British had last been seen retreating. Captain Biddle's battery was deployed at the foot of the hill, at the crossroads, to cover the Portage Road. Surprisingly, in the absence of documents indicating the contrary, Hindman also seemingly left it without close infantry support and somewhat isolated from the main body of troops stationed across the hilltop. With these pieces in place, further inspection of the captured British artillery revealed that the essential hand tools required to load and fire the guns were either broken from the initial fight or were entirely missing. Without these tools, the captured guns were deemed to be unworkable and Ripley ordered Captain McDonald (Nineteenth Regiment) to locate General Brown and get permission to remove the British artillery pieces to the security of the American camp.

Descending the hillside, McDonald almost immediately came upon General Brown and his staff moving up the slope with Jesup's corps. Dismissing the Lieutenant's request on the grounds that "there were matters of more importance to attend to at that moment,"[7] Brown rode onto the hilltop to discuss the tactical situation with Ripley. At the same time, Jesup's regiment began to form on the right of the Twenty-Third Regiment, with its right flank pushed forward to enfilade any British force that might ascend the steeper north slope of the hillside. To the rear of the American position, Porter's reduced brigade of around three hundred men, consisting of the Canadian Volunteers (Lieutenant Colonel Willcocks), Pennsylvania Volunteers (Major Wood), and New York Volunteers (Lieutenant Colonel Dobbin), were now also arriving on the battlefield at the Portage Road. Here they received new orders and were guided across the fields toward the American left flank, which inevitably led them over ground that was littered with the bodies of the dead, dying, and badly wounded from the initial disastrous stands taken by the First Brigade.

Upon their arrival on the western slope of the hill, the Third Brigade formed its line at right angles to the First Regiment, facing due west toward Skinner's Lane. Behind this new two-front line, the captured artillery was left ignored, except for the admiring inspection of some of the American artillerists, including Lieutenant Douglass, who later described his assessment of the guns: "I rode around ... those pieces, to enjoy the satisfaction of seeing and handling them. They were eight in number — brass guns, of the most beautiful model, of different calibres, from six to twenty-four pounders ..."[8]

In discussing matters, the two generals held opposite views of the situation. Ripley was persistent in his assertion that the British would not let the loss of the guns go unchallenged and that a new counterattack was imminent, while Brown was elated at his army's success and was confident the enemy was fleeing from the field. In fact, Brown was so certain in his opinion that he decided to prove the point by making a personal reconnaissance in front of his own lines! Riding up and across the hilltop with his aides, Brown soon saw that Ripley's fears were accurate and he "could no longer doubt, that a more extensive line than he had before seen during the engagement was near and rapidly advancing on us ..."[9] In a show of extreme daring, one of Brown's aides, Captain Spencer, sought to confirm the identity of the approaching force and "without a remark, put spurs to his horse and rode directly up to the advancing lines then turning towards the enemy's right enquired in a firm and strong voice, What Regiment is that? And was as promptly answered The Royal Scotts, Sir ..."[10] In response, General Brown and Captain Spencer "threw themselves in the rear of our troops without loss of time ..."[11] Which is a polite way of saying they got the hell out of there, narrowly avoiding, for a second time in less than an hour, death or capture by the British.

Confirmation of this event also comes from the other side of the lines in the account of Lieutenant Ruttan of the Incorporated Militia:

> At ... about 9 o'clock at night [10:00 p.m. EDT] ... I saw a mounted officer in front of our line but about a company distant

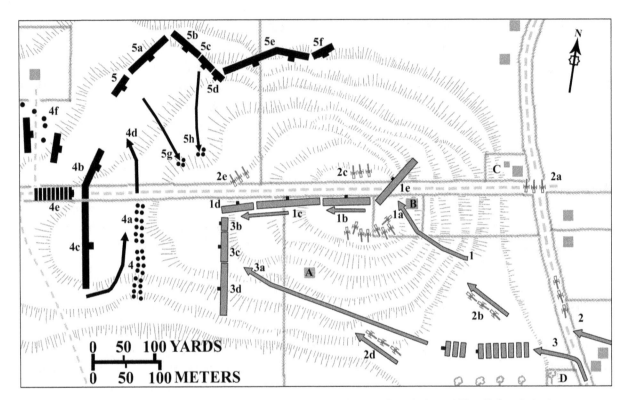

THE AMERICAN THIRD BRIGADE ARRIVES ON THE FIELD AND THE BRITISH REGROUP FOR A MAJOR COUNTERATTACK (CIRCA 10:30–10:50 P.M.)

A. Buchner house
B. Lundy's Lane churchyard
C. Johnson's Tavern
D. Pier's farmstead

American Redeployment

1. The Twenty-Fifth Regiment (1) arrives at the hilltop (1a) as the main American line — Twenty-Third (1b), Twenty-First (1c), and First (1d) — is in the process of redeploying to the west in order to cover more ground. The Twenty-Fifth forms on the right of the American line with its right flank thrown forward (1e).

2. The three U.S. artillery batteries are brought up from the rear. Upon their arrival, Biddle's battery (2) is emplaced at the crossroads (2a). Towson's battery (2b) moves up from Pier's farmstead (D) and is emplaced on the forward (north) slope of the hill, to the right-front (2c) of the Twenty-Third Regiment (1b). Richie's battery (2d) moves up from west of Pier's farmstead orchard and is emplaced in front (2e) of the First Regiment (1d).

3. The U.S. Third Brigade (Porter's militia) (3) enters the field in column and advances directly to the far left flank of the American line (3a). Here it forms a line-of-battle — Canadian Volunteers (3b), New York State militias (3c), Pennsylvania State militias (3d) — at right angles to Lundy's Lane, fronting to the west.

British Redeployment

4. On the British right, the flank companies, 104th (4) and grenadier company 103rd (4a), are initially posted as a skirmish line in front of their main body — right flank 103rd (4b) and 1st (Royal Scots) (4c) — but are then directed to march (4d) to join the assembly of units at the north side of the hill. The 8th (King's) (4e) remains in reserve, while the bulk of the GLI, embodied militias, and Natives (4f) remain out of action at the edge of the field (apart from those already independently acting as couriers, doling out ammunition, and assisting with the wounded).
5. On the north side of the hill, the British units are put into a composite line of regimental companies and detachments (det.) in preparation for an attack on the hilltop: det. Incorporated Militia and 41st (5); Left flank 103rd (5a); 1st (Royal Scots) (5b); det. Incorporated Militia (5c); det. 8th (King's) (5d); 89th (5e); and det. Incorporated Militia (5f). In addition, volunteer parties of men advance to obtain reconnaissance of the enemy's positions (5g, 5h).

on my right and heard him ask in a bold and commanding way "What regiment is this?" The answer was "Scott's Royals Sir." He replied "Very Well, stand you fast Scottish Royals" and disappeared towards the enemy's line.[12]

Seeking to determine the dispositions of the force in front of him before initiating his attack, General Drummond now asked for volunteers to reconnoitre and report back:

Although there was a moon, it was yet as dark as to prevent distinguishing our men from those of the Enemy. We could plainly see [the silhouette on the hilltop of] a line forming in our front and hear every order given. General Drummond, who was immediately behind my company, called for an officer and 20 men to advance and ascertain whether we had a friend or foe in front … [but] being of the opinion that one or two men would execute this order better than twenty, I took Corporal Ferguson … and quietly advanced under a cover of a fence and lying trees until I could discover long tailed coats turned up with white. I could not distinguish blue from scarlet cloth but heard the words "Forward March," words never so combined with us … which convinced us that those in front of us were enemies. Immediately after I turned to retire my steps, a field piece was "Let Off" from the [American] line when their firing at once became general. I fell in with a number of our men, some of whom never lived to return to our lines. Providence however, protected the Corporal and me thus far, but I had but just taken my place in the ranks when I was shot through the right shoulder. I scarcely felt the shock, but was conscious that something unusual was the matter as I was involuntarily brought up on both feet (we were all on one knee) and turned quite around. I had gone but a few steps to the rear when I remembered nothing more until about 2 o'clock the next morning when I found myself lying on my back on the floor of a room being examined by a surgeon who promised me "Done For" …[13]

— Lieutenant Ruttan (Incorporated Militia)

Similarly, Ensign John Lampman's (Incorporated Militia) memoirs later recorded:

During this part of the battle, the British noted a commotion to their front and Lampman was given permission to reconnoitre. He went around the flank of his regiment and concealed himself under the shadow of some trees directly in front of the British line. Soon a cavalcade rode up and halted directly before him. They held a brief conversation and they challenged the army before them, hidden in the darkness…. The night was generally cloudy but as the challenge was being given the moon came out for a moment and he [Lampman] believed it was the Commander of the US Army. The British reply was a furious fire along the whole line and which the enemy made equally furious and sustained fire. Lampman hurried back to his position in the ranks and as he was jumping a fence he had his trousers knee shot through and one of his epaulettes shot off …[14]

CHAPTER 7

A Crucible of Fire: The British Counterattacks

Previously, at the foot of the north side of the hill, and despite suffering from blood loss and pain resulting from his wound, General Drummond had been fully occupied in trying to create some semblance of order from the confusion prevailing in his army since he had lost his second-in-command and his troops had been ejected from the hilltop. Establishing a new line, the British position had shifted west to the point where Drummond's left flank now stood directly north of the position occupied by his centre at the start of the battle. No proper regimental or even company order for units could be created amongst the mass of men gathered at the foot of the hill, but the innate discipline of the troops and the efforts of their NCOs and officers brought forth a strong line, formed in a rough arc and focused on the one place they knew the enemy stood: the hilltop.

No confirmed accurate list of the final lineup exists, but according to Lieutenant Duncan Clark of the Incorporated Militia, it was comprised of "the 89th Regiment and divisions of the 8th Regiment ... three companies of the Incorporated Militia ... stationed in the centre and a party of Royals, 103rd, 104th and 41st Flank companies stationed on the right. At the same time, a division of [at least two companies from] the Incorporated Militia ... wheeled on its left ..."[1]

With his formations in some semblance of order, Drummond awaited his scouts' reports. But as time passed and nothing in the way of information seemed to be coming in, he decided he could not afford to wait any longer and ordered the advance. Inexplicably, despite having lost the guns in the first place due to his failure to provide a light

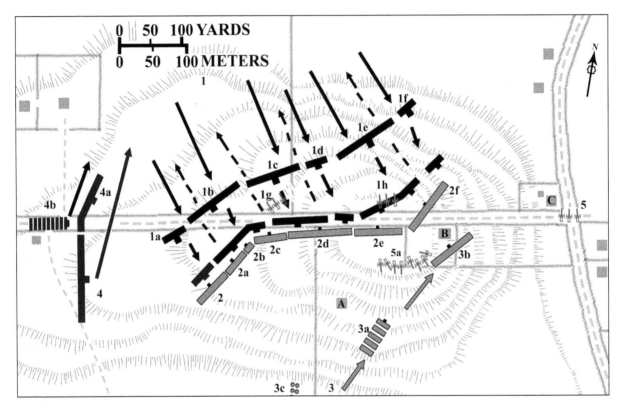

THE FIRST CONSOLIDATED BRITISH COUNTERATTACK TO RETAKE THE CAPTURED GUNS FAILS (CIRCA 10:50–11:30 P.M.)

A. Buchner house
B. Lundy's Lane churchyard
C. Johnson's Tavern

1. From their assembly area at the foot of the north-west foot of the hill (1), the composite British line— det. IMUC (1a); grenadier company 103rd / flank companies 104th / det. 41st (1b); det. IMUC (1c); det. 8th (King's) (d); 89th (1e); det. IMUC (1f) — advances to attack the hilltop. After delivering a succession of volleys from lower down the slope, and with some units on one knee, the line re-forms, advances, and overruns the American hilltop artillery (1g, 1h) before opening fire on the main American line at close range.

2. Across the hilltop, the American line — PA State militias (2); NY State militias (2a); Canadian Volunteers (2b); First (2c); Twenty-First (2d); Twenty-Third (2e); and Twenty-Fifth (2f) — engages the British line. After considerable heavy

fighting at point-blank range, it beats off the first British counterattack for the guns.

3. Winfield Scott's consolidated First Brigade (3) marches up and is initially stationed in column at the foot of the hill (3a), until it moves up and forms a second line (3b) behind the American right flank. Lieutenant Riddle's company (3c), which had been previously detached as a picket line, is left behind at the foot of the hill.

4. Retreating to their original assembly area (1), the British are forced to take time to regroup for a second counterattack. To support this, General Drummond orders the units on the right flank — 1st (Royal Scots) (4); left flank 103rd (4a); and 8th (King's) (4b) — to move up in close support.

5. Biddle's artillery battery (5); captured British artillery battery (5a).

infantry screen, Drummond now repeated this error by not sending out any skirmishers to make contact with the enemy and provide guidance to the formations moving up behind. As a result, the British force moved up the slope, maintaining a disciplined and "profound silence ..."[2] as they approached the equally silent and determined line of American troops.

Having recovered from his unpleasant surprise at finding the British were indeed advancing, General Brown attempted to correct his previous error of judgment by ordering General Porter's troops, stationed at ninety degrees from the rest of the line, to swing forward to face the oncoming

threat. He then rode off to notify General Ripley of the imminent attack.

Initially obeying their commander, Porter and his brigade commander, Major Stanton, were in the process of moving their troops when the major, riding forward of his general and exclaiming "Where are they?"[3] found the source of his inquiry looming out of the darkness and was quickly captured. In response, Porter raced back to his men, halted the redeploying wheel, and prepared to receive the attack with his left flank thrown back and the companies extended to the left to cover more ground.

Beginning with the far right of the American position, the two forces came into contact and began firing. Positioned in front of the American line, Towson's and Ritchie's artillery may have been able to get off a single round of canister ammunition into the British formation, but no more, as the British volleys cut down the gun crews, almost to a man. For the next twenty minutes, the two lines of infantry hammered each other with devastating fire. Orders and directions from officers on one side of the fight could not only be heard, but were occasionally mistakenly obeyed by the enemy troops. Survivors recounted being able to discern details on the enemy's regimental buttons and cap plates, which were illuminated by the intermittent flashes of deadly musket fire. In addition, the varying angles and elevations of the hillside made accurate aiming in the dark difficult, with many volleys being heard to whip over the heads of the soldiers, especially in the case of some of the British units, who, as in the case of Lieutenant Ruttan (quoted above), were firing while down on one knee.

As a final incident of this portion of the engagement, it would also appear that the confusion and deadly peril of the fight raging across the hilltop had either distracted or entirely removed the guards placed on the British prisoners within the small "church" in the graveyard. As a result, they were now able to decamp through a window and disappear into the night, hoping to make their way to the relative safety of their own lines. At the same time, unable to breach the American line and running out of ammunition, the attacking British units were forced to abandon the assault and fell back toward the northwest corner of the hill, there to begin the difficult process of collecting their scattered forces in order to mount another frontal assault.

Certain the British would return, Ripley ordered Porter's brigade to complete its swing forward, thus extending the American line to the west, and facing to the north-northwest. This they did, literally climbing over the British dead and wounded before establishing their new formation. Elsewhere along the American front, while some of the American guns sited ahead of the line-of-battle may have been partially re-manned, the likelihood is that as a result of the virtual elimination of their crews and the death or flight of their horse teams, these guns remained principally as battlefield obstacles rather than as effective weapons of war. Similarly, within the infantry line, the American dead and wounded were pulled back and stripped of their remaining ammunition, while those left standing closed the gaps in their lines, refilled their cartridge boxes with the additional rounds, and drained what little tepid water remained in their canteens — hoping to clear the unpleasant taste of the black powder that filled their mouths.

For nearly half an hour, both forces prepared for the next round of fighting, while General Ripley pressed General Brown to bring up the remains of General Winfield Scott's brigade to bolster the depleted American position. Brown was initially reluctant to make this commitment, preferring to hold Scott's men as a reserve for use in mopping up the enemy once they were finally beaten. However, when Major Leavenworth (Ninth Regiment) arrived with the news that the remnants of Scott's three regiments had been consolidated into a single force and was already at the foot of the hill and ready for use, Brown personally went down the south slope to confer with Scott about the further use of the First Brigade, leaving Ripley in charge of the hilltop defences.

After a short while, Major Leavenworth brought the First Brigade up the hill and began its deployment as a reserve, a short distance behind the right flank of the American line. At the same time, the British appeared out of the darkness and the duel of musketry began once more. According to Colonel Leavenworth, "their near approach was discovered by a sheet of flame from both armies — who were not more than 30 yards [27 meters] distant from each other & nearly in parallel lines."[4] According to several accounts, this round of fighting was even more desperate and devastating than the first, as sections of the lines converged, resulting in hand-to-hand combat.

This new British attack now began to tell on the American units. On the left, Porter's militia began to waver, especially Willcocks's Canadian Volunteers, who were under no illusion of the fate that awaited them if they were captured. Under a heavy fire, this unit soon broke ranks, heading for the rear, followed almost immediately by numbers of men from the Pennsylvania and New York militia regiments. In response, the regulars from the First Regiment swung back, anchoring the corner and partially preventing the British units on that flank from taking advantage of this withdrawal by pressing forward with a charge. Meanwhile, a strong effort by the militia officers behind the American line prevented a total collapse of this flank and stabilized the position, re-forming a diminished line virtually where it had started, facing west toward Skinner's Lane.

Similarly, in the centre, the Twenty-First and Twenty-Third Regiments had wide gaps blown in their line, causing some men to edge back and break ranks. It was entirely possible that the American line could have broken at this point, except for the personal intervention of General Ripley, who worked tirelessly to steady his troops. Finally, on the right flank, Jesup's corps were taking a heavy pounding, but had remained in position, even though their commander had by now been wounded three times and was in extreme pain. Behind Jesup's line, Winfield Scott was determined to make up for his earlier costly stand before the British guns, having decided that a strong counter-attack on the British line would rout the enemy.

Calling on Leavenworth to re-form his consolidated line back into a column, Scott was forced to wait as the sections moved into place. He then led the depleted First Brigade forward, passing through a gap in the American line near Towson's abandoned guns and crossing Lundy's Lane, heading for the British line. Almost immediately, the American column came under heavy British fire. Suffering casualties, the column veered left, away from the deadly fire, and marched west, directly along Lundy's Lane — between the two opposing lines!

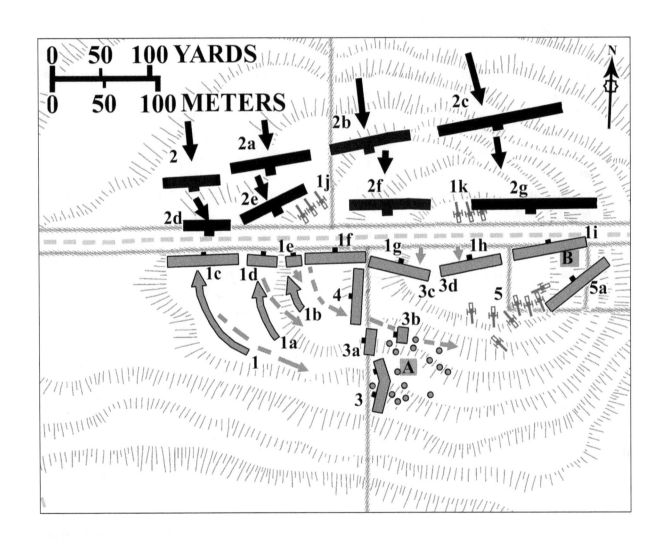

THE INITIAL PHASE OF THE BRITISH SECOND CONSOLIDATED COUNTERATTACK AND THE PARTIAL COLLAPSE OF THE AMERICAN LEFT FLANK (CIRCA 11:30–11:45 P.M.)

A. Buchner house
B. Lundy's Lane churchyard

1. General Porter's Third Brigade — PA State militias (1); NY State militias (1a); and Canadian Volunteers (1b) — initially positioned with its left flank refused, swing forward (1c, 1d, 1e) to extend and stabilize the already established American regimental line — the First (1f); Twenty-First (1g); Twenty-Third (1h); and Twenty Fifth (1i). However, the two artillery batteries (1j, 1k) remain effectively abandoned.
2. After having previously regrouped and established a new composite line, believed to be composed of det. IMUC (2); amalgamated detachments det. 1st (Royal Scots) / Flank companies 104th / grenadier company 103rd / 41st (2a); amalgamated detachments det. IMUC /det. 8th (King's) (2b); and 89th (2c), the British line again advances up the hill and opens fire with volleys while still on the slope. It then advances to the hillcrest and makes a second stand (2d, 2e, 2f, 2g), exchanging fire with the American line across the width of Lundy's Lane.
3. Under heavy pressure from the right flank of the British attack (2d, 2e), Porter's Third Brigade — PA State militias (1c); NY State militias (1d); and Canadian Volunteers (1e) — begins to crumble and withdraws, but is successfully halted and begins to re-form (3, 3a, 3b). Similarly, elements of the Twenty-First (1g) and Twenty-Third (1h) are forced back (3c, 3d), partially disorganizing the American front line.
4. As the British right flank (2d, 2e) presses forward, the First Regiment (1f) wheels backward on its right (4) to secure the flank and link up with the regrouping Third Brigade.
5. The captured British artillery line (5) becomes disordered as attempts are made to move the guns. Winfield Scott's composite unit of the First Brigade (5a) remains uncommitted behind the American front line during the initial phase of the second British counterattack.

Despite Scott's later insistence that he had notified the regimental commanders of the Twenty-Third, Twenty-First, and First Regiments of his intentions, the message seemingly failed to get through to the front line, for seeing an unknown target immediately in front of them, the men of the Second Brigade unleashed a volley into the First Brigade's column. Recoiling away to the right, Winfield Scott's corps was hit by yet another volley from the opposing British line, forcing it back again to the left. There was nowhere for the men of the First Brigade to go but forward as they now ran the gauntlet of repeated point-blank fire from the two opposing lines. Both Scott and Leavenworth had their horses shot out from under them, forcing the two leaders to continue under this storm of fire on foot. Inevitably, these blows became too much for the men in the column and they broke, continuing west along Lundy's Lane until they passed the left flank of the American line, where they were able to work their way southwest and halt partway down

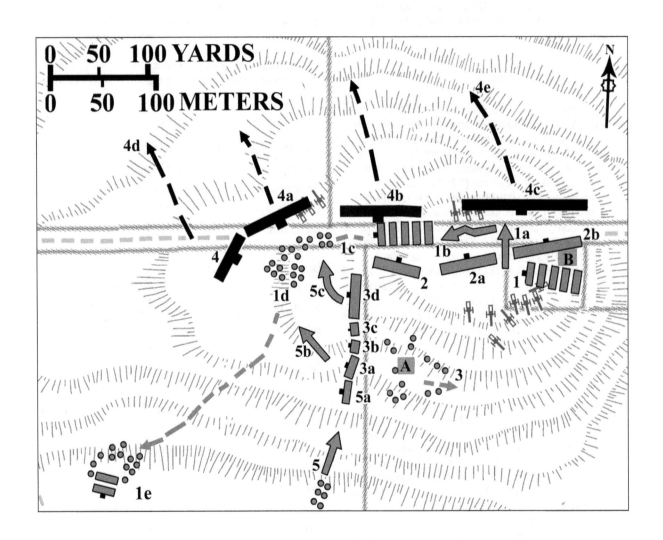

THE SECOND PHASE OF THE BRITISH SECOND CONSOLIDATED COUNTERATTACK AND WINFIELD SCOTT'S DISASTROUS COUNTERATTACK. (CIRCA 11:45 P.M.–12:15 A.M.)

A. Buchner house
B. Lundy's Lane churchyard

1. General Winfield Scott decides to use his consolidated brigade to break through the British left flank. Re-forming his column (1), Scott's force passes through the American line (1a) but is hit by heavy British fire and veers left (west) (1b). His column then runs the gauntlet of fire from both lines and breaks (1c). Once the routed men have passed the left flank of the American line (1d) they flee to the rear, only to then begin to re-form (1e) near Skinner's Lane.
2. The main American line — Twenty-First (2); Twenty-Third (2a); and Twenty-Fifth (2b) Regiments.
3. On the American left flank, while individuals leave the field (3), the Third Brigade — PA State militias (3a); NY State militias (3b); and Canadian Volunteers (3c), supported by the First Regiment (3d) — re-form a line-of-battle facing west.
4. The second British counterattack — det. IMUC (4); det. 1st (Royal Scots) / flank companies 104th / grenadier company 103rd / 41st (4a); det. IMUC / det. 8th (King's) (4b); 89th (4c) — fails to break the American line and retires (4d, 4e) to the northwest of the hill where it regroups for a third attack.
5. Lieutenant Riddle's company (Nineteenth Regiment) (5) moves up from the foot of the hill and joins the Third Brigade line (5a). The American left wing then wheels forward (5b, 5c) to re-establish the American line on Lundy's Lane.

the hill. Impressively, many of the few remaining survivors of the First Brigade did not quit the field at this point, but allowed themselves to be halted and begin to re-form what remained of their shattered composite companies. Across the hilltop, the firing continued unabated, but the British were seemingly unable to make the final push that would collapse the American line. Gradually, the British units began to again run short of ammunition and once they were unable to return the American fire, were either forced to withdraw or simply melted away into the night.

By this point, both armies were drained of manpower and ammunition to the point of almost total exhaustion. On the hilltop, large gaps existed between the company-sized formations that earlier had counted themselves as regiments. Consequently, the Americans were, once again, reduced to searching the bodies at their feet to recover sufficient rounds for their muskets. In fact, the Twenty-Fifth Regiment had lost so many men that it was unable to maintain a formation in two ranks and was forced to create its line one-man deep. On the other flank, Porter's depleted and wavering militiamen were "stiffened" when Lieutenant Riddle's company of Nineteenth regular troops appeared out the darkness (having finally realized they had been abandoned by Scott when he marched his brigade toward the hill and were therefore no longer needed as a picket). As a result, this unit formed at the end of the militia line. And yet again the Third Brigade and the First Regiment picked their way through the prone bodies of their former comrades and the enemy as they wheeled up to the right and formed their new line roughly parallel to the south side of Lundy's Lane.

At the foot of the hill, Drummond's force was in no better a shape, as the cumulative efforts of the day's marching to the field of action, followed by more than five hours of almost continuous battle, had exhausted the troops. More importantly, most of the men from both armies had used up whatever water they had carried and were parched. The fact that the sound of the torrent of the great falls and its endless supply of refreshment, located less than a mile away, could be clearly heard must have been a torment for the wounded and uninjured alike.

Despite his wound, and the two previous failures to recapture the hilltop, General Drummond decided to risk one more attempt. Unfortunately, there is no solid documentation to show to what degree (or if at all) he included those regiments that remained on the British right flank, in reserve, or those that had been re-forming in the rear. All that can be said with certainty is that he pressed his troops into composite units and again established a line facing in the one direction he knew the enemy could be found — on the hill. From the foot of the hill, Drummond's dogged British and Canadian

veterans — for no one could claim there were novices in the British line by this time — marched up the slope once more toward the waiting Americans. According to Jesup, on the right of the American line, this third assault "was now more obstinate than in any of the previous attacks of the enemy — for half an hour, the blaze of the muskets of the two lines mixed …"[5] But despite suffering heavy casualties, especially amongst the officer corps, the American right flank held firm.

Similarly, on the left of the American line, the British force advanced, while having to step on or clamber over the bodies on the ground in a final attempt to come to grips with the Americans. As the combatants began to trade volleys, Winfield Scott once again attempted to make his mark by ordering his partially re-formed remnant of a brigade to advance out from the relative security of the ground on the south side of the hill, near Skinner's Lane, in order to attack the advancing British right flank. Hearing this order, some men of the First Brigade simply slipped off into the darkness. Nevertheless, enough formed in column to satisfy the general and he led them forward once more. Unfortunately for Winfield Scott, he failed to notice that a body of enemy troops (companies from the 104th and Incorporated Militia regiments) were stationed behind a fence line that bordered Lundy's Lane to the left of his advancing column. According to Lieutenant Duncan Clark of the Incorporated Militia, after letting the leading part of the column pass by the British and Canadian troops "kneeled sufficiently low to prevent being seen by the enemy; and when [the Americans came] within a few paces of the British line a signal was given to fire, when both sides were soon engaged in a conflict obstinate beyond description, disorder and dispute was the consequence ..."[6]

In Brown's later analysis of events, this fire disrupted Scott's column at about its centre and caused it to split and recoil "with one part passing to the rear, while the other marched by the right flank of platoons toward the main line ..."[7]; Major Leavenworth simply chose to record that Scott advanced on the British right, "but finding that flank supported by a heavy second line, his charge was withdrawn ..."[8] However, during the subsequent post-war controversy over the overall failure of the 1814 campaign, a less benign analysis was made by the American general, James Wilkinson, who went to great lengths to obtain depositions and sworn testimonies from eyewitnesses and participants in the various events on the Niagara in 1814 as corroborating evidence for his subsequent damning, if biased, critique of the campaign. According to his version of events:

As General Scott led his column down the lane ... General Brown shewed himself on the hill in quest of the Brigadier ... and passed several sections in pursuit of him [Scott], when the column received a volley in its flank from the enemy who were posted behind the fence (the diagram shews it on the left) and then this exhausted, worn out handful of brave men, broke and retreated in disorder; leaving behind them Captain Pentland, who was wounded, with Lieutenant Perry, who was made prisoner, and the curses of their general, who perceiving that his word of command "BATTALION, LEFT WHEEL INTO LINE, QUICK MARCH," was no longer heeded by his wearied and almost heart-broken ranks, exclaimed in a voice of thunder, "THEN YOU MAY ALL GO TO HELL" ...[9]

At this point, Scott seemingly rode away from his men and disappeared into the darkness. Inevitably, abandoned by their leader in the face of the enemy and while under heavy fire, the column was broken and scattered. As Scott's few remaining men fled past to the rear, Porter's troops took up the brunt of the fighting on the American left flank and traded volleys with the British line. It was also at this time that General Brown, who had fallen back with Scott's routed men, suffered

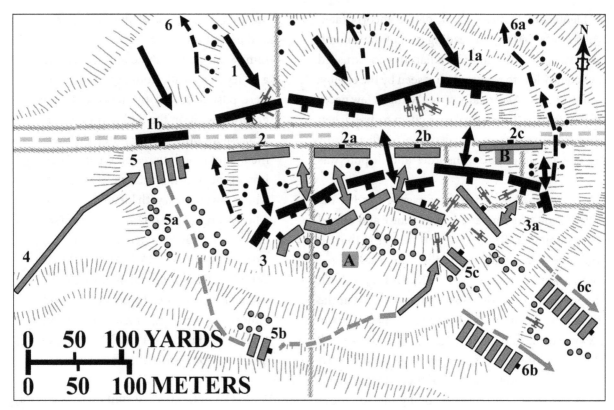

THE THIRD CONSOLIDATED BRITISH COUNTERATTACK TO RETAKE THE GUNS AND BATTLE AFTERMATH (CIRCA 12:25–1:30 A.M.)

A. Buchner house
B. Lundy's Lane churchyard

(*N.B.* Due to imprecise and conflicting accounts, the placement, strength, and composition of the units in this phase can only be considered as an educated estimate, as are the timings of this final combat and aftermath.)

1. The re-formed British line, made up of unidenti-fied composite and ad-hoc companies (off map), advance (1-1a) on the American line. On the right flank, an identified division composed of Incorporated Militia (IMUC) and 104th regimental detachments (1b) takes up a kneeling position behind a fence and hedge that line Lundy's Lane, in order to secure the British flank.

2. The American line, estimated to be made up of a composite of the following: Riddle's company (Nineteenth)/ NY State militias / PA State militias / Canadian Volunteers/ det. First (2); Twenty-First

(2a); Twenty-Third (2b); and Twenty-Fifth in a single rank (2c), line the south side of Lundy's Lane.

3. Under the British attack, the American line is forced back. In heavy hand-to-hand fighting, the hillside becomes a melee of individual battles between detachments and companies, with no defined or identifiable locations (3–3a).

4. Looking to attack the British right flank, General Winfield Scott orders the reorganized remnants of his First Brigade (4) to advance, but fails to spot the kneeling British units (1b).

5. The composite IMUC and 104th (1b) fire into Scott's column (5) at point-blank range, causing it to waver and then break (5a). After retreating, it is rallied and reorganizes yet again (5b). It is then brought up to the hilltop as the fighting ends and is posted on the American right flank (5c).

6. Unable to capitalize on their attack and recapture the guns, British units begin to independently withdraw in various states of discipline and order (6–6a) to positions 500 yards (300 meters) to the north of the hill, where they remain for the night, The Americans remain on the hill between 30 and 60 minutes before making an orderly withdrawal to Chippawa (6b, 6c), leaving behind most of the artillery pieces from both sides.

a wound near his groin (an injury that Brown later complained he "got … through the damned rashness and folly of Scott"),[10] while his aide, Captain Spencer, was killed. Despite their success in driving off Scott's attack, this British force on the right flank, almost out of ammunition and possibly fearing another American offensive, failed to advance to support the main attacks to their left by closing

on the American line. This opening encouraged Porter to initiate a local counterattack of his own, which pushed the exhausted British troops on this flank back once more to the northern slope of the hill before they disengaged and withdrew down the slope into the darkness.

By now, the only fighting still going on was at the centre of both lines. Here the British had succeeded in closing with the American line, and in the case of at least one company of the 41st Regiment (Captain Glew), had driven it back, first by volleys of point-blank fire and then at the point of the bayonet, across the top of the hill and into the midst of the disordered line of artillery. Here the fighting degenerated into fierce hand-to-hand combat. This counterattack almost succeeded, but the inability of the two British flank attacks to break through the American line left the centre unsupported, and there were no reserves left at the foot of the hill that could be pushed forward to swing the balance. Eventually, after suffering additional heavy casualties, the British centre was forced to break off and retire, leaving behind the guns they had almost regained, because there were no ropes and harnesses available to haul them off — a problem that was later to prove even more embarrassing for the Americans.

On the American right flank, General Scott appeared out of the darkness alongside the Twenty-Fifth Regiment, apparently uninjured, despite having been in the thick of the battle from the outset and seeing most of his battalion fall as casualties because of his command decisions. However, the general's personal luck was about to run out; for as he stood talking to Jesup, behind the American line, and as the British were in the process of retiring, a musket ball took the general in the left shoulder, flinging him to the ground. What they were discussing is not recorded; however, given Scott's previous determinations to repeatedly go on the offensive with whatever force he could command, there has been conjecture it might have been the prospect of making a new counterattack with the Twenty-Fifth Regiment.

There is also the intriguing but speculative question of, given the location (behind the American lines and on the reverse slope of the hill) and timing (as the British were supposedly retiring), just where the disabling shot came from. Especially given that for the past five hours Scott had been under constant enemy fire and had not received a scratch — while by contrast, his entire brigade had been shot to pieces.

As the fighting slowly subsided, the Americans held to their final positions across the hill, roughly in the shape of three sides of a box, with the captured British guns in the centre and the American artillery pieces outside of this position some small distance to the north. The casualties, both dead and wounded, as well as those who had sought the safety of the rear during the conflict, had depleted the American numbers to the point that neither Brown, his staff, nor the majority of his surviving regimental commanders were under any illusion that they could withstand another attack of the intensity of the last. In fact, "in a conversation which occurred a few minutes afterwards between Genl. Brown & Majors McRee & Wood and two or three other officers; it was the unanimous belief of all that we had nothing more to fear from the enemy with whom we had been contending; But it appeared to be admitted by everyone that it would be judicious to retire to camp ..."[11]

Pressed to withdraw from the field and have his wounds tended to, Brown relented and rode from his post behind Porter's (left flank) section of the line, toward the right flank, where he came upon Major Leavenworth assembling the skeleton remnants of the First Brigade behind and to the right of the Twenty-Fifth Regimental position. Asking for Winfield Scott, to pass over the command of the army into his hands, he was informed that the general had already preceded him in leaving the field as a result of his wound. This information was then confirmed by Jesup, leaving Brown with no alternative but to relinquish command to General Ripley; but where Ripley was, no one could say. In fact, General Ripley was exactly where he should have been, namely with the remnants of his brigade forming the front face of the box at the centre of the American position.

Following the third assault, Ripley was particularly concerned that another attack would result in the retaking of the guns by the British. To prevent this happening, he prevailed on Porter to detach a force of men to drag off the captured guns. Without horses or proper drag ropes, the already exhausted militiamen started in their assigned duty, manhandling the massive pieces across the rough ground and down the south side of the hill. In this way the battery was further scattered across the hillside. Possibly only one piece, a brass 6-pounder, actually reached the bottom of the slope before the men rebelled: "[B]eing tired out and half dead for want of water, the most of our faces scorched with powder, we refused to do any more ..."[12]

After leaving the field, General Brown later recorded that he met with Major Hindman of the artillery and instructed him to bring off the guns. In addition, that he:

> Saw many scattering men on the road — not a man was running away nor appeared to be afraid, but having lost their officers and suffering intensely from thirst, were either drinking or seeking ... water. This scene confirmed the Maj. Genl. in the belief that it was proper for the Army to return to camp.... An officer was accordingly sent to say to Genl. Ripley that the Army would return to camp ...[13]

However, this message failed to reach Ripley for some time.

With his own directives received directly from Brown, Hindman immediately returned to the positions of his batteries to oversee their removal to the camp at Chippawa. Biddle's battery at the crossroads was relatively untouched, as it had been isolated from the fighting on the hilltop. It was therefore soon limbered up by its crew and on the move — picking up on the way the British 6-pounder left by Porter's militia at the foot of the hill.

Upon the hilltop, the situation was significantly different. All of the American and British battery horses and gun crews were either dead or missing, and the guns stood undefended on the north side of Lundy's Lane, well in front of the retired American defensive position. Hindman therefore collected whatever artillerymen or soldiers he could muster and proceeded to wheel off the majority of Towson's and Ritchie's guns by hand, hauling them first into Lundy's Lane and then east, down the slope toward the crossroads with the Portage Road. But without enough men to complete the job in a single effort, Hindman was forced to leave behind one of his own 6-pounder guns, a howitzer, and two ammunition wagons, as well as the remaining British artillery pieces, for what was expected to be a second trip.

Uninformed of the departure of both Brown and Winfield Scott, and unable to see the actions of Hindman due to the darkness, Ripley maintained his line of defence on the south side of the crest of the hill for over half an hour after the final British counterattack had ended. He also ordered the collection and removal of as many of the wounded as possible while he looked for new orders. When they eventually arrived, they handed him the command of the army, while simultaneously directing him to withdraw to Chippawa. Ripley was now placed in the difficult position of either disobeying a direct order and remaining in control of the hill — with a diminished force and under threat of further attack by an enemy of unknown strength — or obeying and abandoning the ground so desperately fought over for the past few hours.

Calling a Council of Officers, Ripley found that only General Porter was adamant of the need to retain the ground, while the remainder felt that they could not survive another attack and that withdrawal was essential and in accordance with General Brown's specific commands. Still undecided, Ripley was then informed that Hindman had already withdrawn his guns from in front of the American position. This information swung the balance and the decision was made to quietly withdraw, much to the disgust of General Porter.

The surviving troops formed composite units and then marched from the field, passing as they did so a small detachment of around fifty men, drawn from the Twenty-First and Twenty-Third Regiments (Second Brigade). These men had been on camp duties when the Second Brigade had marched, but had been brought up during the latter part of the night's fight by Major Morill Marston (Twenty-First Regiment). However, before they could enter the battle, they had met with General Brown retiring from the field. Brown had instructed Marston to remain on the Portage Road and act as rearguard for the army.[14]

As a result, once the main body had passed, the only American troops remaining on the field were stragglers and small detachments being used to bring away as many of the wounded as they could find. However, without Hindman or his artillerists, no effort was made by the infantry to see that Ripley's earlier order to remove the British guns had been completed. Hindman, on the other hand, did attempt to return for the remaining guns by sending forward a detachment of artillerymen and wagon drivers to prepare at least one of the British 24-pounder pieces for transportation, while he attempted to locate spare horses and bring them up to haul off the prizes. When he returned, he found that the guns and at least part of his detachment had been overrun and captured by the British, forcing him to retreat as quietly as possible in the direction of the American camp. During this journey, Hindman met Towson, who was also returning with horses on a similar errand. Apprising Towson that the hill and the guns were once again in the hands of the British, the two officers gave up their attempt and returned to the American camp, where they were immediately engaged in preparing defences for an anticipated British attack on that position at dawn.[15]

On the British side of the hill, the troops were, if anything, even more exhausted and thirsty than their American counterparts. Most of them had been on the move since sunrise and had undertaken a gruelling march before engaging in several hours of combat. Furthermore, after three devastating assaults on the hilltop, the failure to recapture the guns had demoralized the troops to such an extent that there was no question of there being a fourth attempt. General Drummond was also faced with the fact that during the third assault, the Americans had been able to undertake a counterattack with a column of troops. Admittedly this had been beaten off, but it left the question of what additional reserves the Americans had available for another attack, for there were none in the British force to stop them. Fully expecting the battle to continue with an American advance from the hilltop within the next hour, or as soon as daylight returned, General Drummond, wounded as he was, retained command and ordered the majority of his surviving troops to withdraw some five hundred yards (300 meters) north and re-form.

For the remainder of the night, the hilltop of Lundy's Lane was relatively unoccupied by the two armies, except for the wounded and the dead; it therefore fell to the initiative of individual British commanders to move their men forward and establish a picket line to warn of any American advance. For example, men from the 104th Regiment advanced and reoccupied the crest of the hill. They then used the carcasses of the dead artillery horses to create a protective barrier in case of attack, before attempting to bring succour to the American and British wounded that lay around them. One officer from this regiment, Lieutenant John LeCouteur, later wrote:

> I was on duty that night, what a dismal night. There were three hundred dead on the Niagara side of the hillock, and about a hundred of ours, besides several hundred wounded. The miserable badly wounded were groaning or imploring us for water, the Indians prowling about them and scalping or plundering…. Our

Men's heads and those of the Americans were within a few yards of each other at this spot, so close had been the deadly strife at this point.... The scene in the morning was not more pleasant than the night's horrors. We had to wait on our slaughterhouse till 11 before we got a mouthful [to eat] ...[16]

In a similar manner, men from the 89th Regiment moved up onto the hill and beyond. Interestingly, while General Drummond and others referred to a charge being made by a company of the 41st Regiment (Captain Glew) that recaptured the guns, this later action by the 89th would correspond with Hindman's eyewitness account of the post-battle recapturing of the British guns and the American detachment sent to retrieve them. As a result, it is possible that elements of these two separate events became either accidentally or deliberately intermingled in the official reports on the battle.

This revision of events and substitution of units also served a secondary purpose by obscuring the fact that the 41st attack had been pushed back from its position on top of the hill during the battle and made it appear the guns had been recaptured permanently and as part of the earlier British counterattacks against the main American force in line, and not in the aftermath of the fighting and against a smaller team of men occupied in removing the guns.

Returning to the American camp, Ripley was shocked to see that there were numerous troops (possibly a thousand) who had not been brought to the battlefield as previously ordered and who could have probably swung the course of the battle if they had! Seeking out the wounded General Brown at his tent, Ripley reported on the withdrawal and, despite having officially taken charge of the army, allowed Brown to direct him as to the disposition of the army for the following day.

Considering the circumstances and events surrounding this action, it is not surprising that the official reports of both Major General Brown and Lieutenant General Drummond were highly coloured by the necessity of avoiding censure for mistakes made during the day's buildup to the battle, not to mention the confusion of the night action, the loss of the prized guns by both forces, and the failure of either army to take any decisive offensive action to press the supposed victory that both generals claimed for their respective armies. What is undeniable, however, are the heavy casualties suffered by both armies and the savage intensity of the fighting that took place on the hill at Lundy's Lane.[*17, *18] (See chart on page 144.)

As already mentioned, in later months the circumstances surrounding the leaving of the cannon and failure of the American campaign on the Niagara became a major cause of controversy within the American military. It was also extensively reported on in the press, creating something of a public scandal as numerous contradictory depositions and letters were written and published in support of either Brown or Ripley. In fact, matters went so far as to see an official Court of Inquiry established on Ripley's conduct. However, political considerations and, according to some American reports, pressure directly from Winfield Scott, once again halted an official inquiry before too many potentially critical and embarrassing facts could be revealed about Brown and Scott's command decisions that night. Interestingly, this apparent "cover-up" prompted one military champion of Ripley, General James Wilkinson, to later make the following two dramatic statements in his 1816 published critique of the campaign:

> With a single remark, I shall dismiss this dateless official letter of General Brown.... Whoever will take the pains to examine and compare it with the facts ... will find it more abundant in *fictions* and *falsehoods* than any public document of equal length extant in our language.[19]

> ...That by the incompetency of General Brown, and the inconsiderate rashness and folly of General Scott on the 25th of July, 1814, a body of gallant troops ... were committed to a destructive action, under every circumstance of disadvantage; that the artillery of the enemy, won by their valor ... were through the ignorance and remissness of the commanding general, left on the field of battle ...[20]

Despite such ringing condemnations, such was the weight of Washington's "official" opinion, bolstered by the published campaign memoirs of Brown and Scott, that the impression left to historians has tended to lay much of the criticism upon Ripley.

OFFICIAL CASUALTY FIGURES, BATTLE OF LUNDY'S LANE, JULY 25, 1814[17]

British
British Regulars
Killed:	5 Officers, 72 Other Ranks
Wounded:	23 Officers, 456 Other Ranks
Known Prisoners:	6 Officers, 18 Other Ranks
Missing:	4 Officers, 106 Other Ranks

Canadian Militia
Killed:	1 Officer, 7 Other Ranks
Wounded:	13 Officers, 49 Other Ranks
Known Prisoners:	3 Officers, 14 Other Ranks
Missing:	2 Officers, 77 Other Ranks

Cavalry
Wounded:	1 Other Rank
Missing:	1 Other Rank

Artillery
Wounded:	1 Officer, 15 Other Ranks
Missing:	8 Other Ranks

Native Allies
Numbers not known

OFFICIAL CASUALTY FIGURES, BATTLE OF LUNDY'S LANE, JULY 25, 1814[18]

American
First Brigade (Winfield Scott)
Killed:	109 All Ranks
Wounded:	350 All Ranks
Missing and Prisoner:	57 All Ranks
Total:	416 All Ranks

Plus 200 slightly wounded but not disabled

Combined Second Brigade (Ripley), Third Brigade (Porter)
Killed:	64 (173)* All Ranks
Wounded:	220 (571)* All Ranks
Missing and Prisoner:	60 (117)* All Ranks
Total:	344 (861)*All Ranks

Plus 75 slightly wounded but not disabled

Artillery
Killed:	10 All Ranks
Wounded:	35 All Ranks
Missing:	1 All Ranks
Total:	46 All Ranks

Cavalry
Killed:	1 All Ranks
Wounded:	2 All Ranks

N.B. For details on the numbers marked * see Notes.

CHAPTER 8

Back Where We Started

As daylight returned and visibility increased on the morning of July 26, 1814, the intensity of the night's carnage became apparent to the British pickets, with the crest of the hill being literally covered with opposing lines of bodies, marking where the regimental formations had stood, fought, and died, sometimes within feet of each other. Expecting the Americans to rejoin the action at dawn, General Drummond formed his surviving troops in the fields north of the hill and marched them up the slope once more. To his surprise and relief, his advance pickets reported that there was no sign of American formations, leaving Drummond's army free to reoccupy the hilltop unopposed. Even more pleasing was the discovery that not only had most of the captured British artillery been found scattered across the hillside, but in addition, two American pieces were lying abandoned and ready for use.

Needing to know how the Americans were planning to follow up on the night's action, Drummond dispatched Captain John Norton and his Native warriors to locate and report on the dispositions and status of the enemy. He also directed his troops to spread out across the fields and find the wounded who had survived the night in order to remove them for treatment at Fort George. There was also the less pleasant duty of collecting the bodies of the dead for burial. Initially interring the dead in individual graves or long trenches, the large numbers of casualties soon made it apparent that this work would take days rather than hours. Concerned that the Americans would return to rejoin the fight, and partially due to a (false) rumour

The south (L) and north (R) faces of the Lundy's Lane battlefield monument and crypt, 2013. Located at the highest point in the hilltop cemetery and dedicated in 1895, this mausoleum has become the final resting place for the remains of soldiers from both sides that have become unearthed in the surrounding area during the last two centuries.

that the Americans had cremated the bodies of the British and Canadian dead after Chippawa, a difficult and subsequently controversial decision was made for the disposal of the remaining bodies on the hilltop. From this point, the order was given to only bury those bodies identified as British and Canadian while the remainder were to be cremated. This was an unfortunate necessity of war that was later used by the American press as grounds to cite the inhumanity and bestiality of the

Above: Four grave markers dedicated to at least twenty-one U.S. troops killed within sight of this spot on the night of July 25, 1814.

Left: A bronze statue located alongside the principal battle monument in the Lundy's Lane hilltop cemetery.

British soldiery, as cremation was not a common military burial practice at that time. On this matter, Lieutenant Duncan Clark of the Incorporated Militia recorded:

The British troops were now in possession of the battlefield, the remainder of the night and the whole of the next day was employed in burying their own dead and burning those of the enemy which were collected and piled up on the hill in three heaps, sometimes upwards of 30 lifeless bodies, each with layers of dried oak rails, the torch was applied and the whole reduced to ashes ...[1]

This necessity was also recorded in the memoirs of Ensign Lampman (Incorporated Militia), revealing another aspect of this event and typifying the well-documented black humour of survivors of battles:

> As Lampman and another officer were strolling in view of the burning pyre, they came across a dead enemy soldier. One of them said that the man should be in the fire because he was fat and would burn well. Just then a musket, which had been thrown into the fire, went off and the bullet struck at the officer's feet, showering them with sand. They agreed that when the dead Yankees began to shoot, it was time for them to retreat, and they retreated ..."[2]

As expected, an American force appeared on the Chippawa road later that morning and the British troops formed their line-of-battle. However, the Americans gave no indication of having any inclination to fight and soon withdrew once more toward Chippawa, leaving the British in control of the strategic hilltop.

This reluctance on the part of the Americans to re-engage the British became a further source of controversy and recriminations in the annals of several of the major personalities involved in the night's action, as well as amongst military historians down to the present day. However, American documents written at the time clearly indicate that apart from General Brown, lying wounded in his tent, virtually none of the other senior or regimental commanders had any doubt that despite having gained the upper hand during the night's fighting, the strategic advantage had been lost to the British by obeying Brown's orders to abandon the hill and fall back on the defensive at Chippawa. Furthermore, they believed the heavy casualties and current state of the American army left it effectively incapable of successfully rejoining the fight with the British, who it was believed had been reinforced and now significantly outnumbered them.

> From what I saw of our forces, which I do not think at the time exceeded 1500 or 1600 men, and from what I had seen of the enemy's force the preceding evening, I did think it the most consummate folly to attempt to regain possession of the field of battle — and every officer with whom I conversed, among whom were many of the first distinction, expressed their astonishment at such an attempt and their surprise that every exertion

was not made immediately to take up the line of march for Fort Erie ..."

— Colonel Leavenworth,
Ninth Regiment, January 15, 1815[3]

According to General Brown's later version of events, once the army had returned to camp, he gave General Ripley clear orders to "Organize his Battalions ... and put himself, with all the men he could muster, of every Corps, on the field of battle as the day dawned, there to be governed by circumstances; at all events to bring off the captured cannon ..."[4] What he failed to mention, however, is that to do as he had been ordered, Ripley would have been forced to "allow the enfeebled troops barely one hour and fifty minutes to cook, eat, clean and refresh themselves, to draw ammunition, put their arms in order for action, and make a march, which ... required an hour the evening before, when the troops were fresh ..."[5]

As a result, while Ripley obeyed Brown's orders, he appears to have taken his time about establishing his force. This delay infuriated Brown, whose later version of events stated: "As day approached, finding that the columns had not moved, Genl. Brown ordered his staff to go to every commanding officer of Corps and order them to be promptly prepared to march in obedience to the order given to Genl. Ripley but it was

sunrise [around 6:00 a.m. EDT] before the Army crossed the Chippawa ..."[6]

Once across the bridge, Ripley left a third of his force in reserve, while the remainder advanced to the hamlet of Bridgewater Mills. From this point, only detachments from the Twenty-Third (Lieutenant Tappan) and Nineteenth (Lieutenant Riddle) Regiments were detailed to probe forward and make a reconnaissance of the British positions. Reporting back, Tappan claimed the British were in strength on the hill and alert to any possible attack.

I was ordered by Gen. Ripley, in conjunction with Lieut. Riddle of the 19th infantry, to proceed with our respective companies through the woods on our left, advance towards the enemy, and reconnoitre his position, strength and movements. His order was executed. On unmasking from the woods, we discovered the enemy posted on a height, about a mile in advance on the ground where we left him. His whole battery was planted on an eminence upon the right of the road; his left extended in line, so far as I could see, through an orchard towards the Niagara, by which that flank was undoubtedly protected. His right was in column near the battery, in force, apparently more than sufficient when displayed into line, to extend to a wood, difficult to be penetrated…. His position was commanding, his flanks well covered, his centre impenetrable, unassailable, and it would, in my humble opinion have been an act of rashness, bordering on insanity to have attempted an attack …"

— Lieutenant Tappan, Twenty-Third Regiment, March 20, 1815[7]

Satisfied that he had done as ordered, Ripley held a conference of his fellow senior officers and solicited their advice. All agreed that any attempt to initiate an attack would be folly and that remaining on the defensive was the only practical alternative. The question was where to make their stand.

The obvious choice was to hold the south bank of the Chippawa. However, such was the concern over the state of the army and the potential movement of Drummond's force around the American flank that a split in opinion developed, with a slight majority coming down in favour of a retreat to the vicinity of Fort Erie. Ripley went one step further and proposed the evacuation of the army back across the Niagara River to Buffalo; but when Porter and most of the other officers vehemently opposed this move (which they argued could only be interpreted as an open admission of defeat),

TROOP MOVEMENTS, JULY 26–AUGUST 2, 1814

1. July 26: U.S. forces, under Brigadier General Ripley, advance from their encampment at Chippawa (1) to Bridgewater. From here, only a small reconnaissance force (1a) advance to observe the British positions on the Lundy's Lane hilltop. Convinced any further offensive would be futile, they return back the way they had come to Chippawa, burning the community of Bridgewater as they leave. Subsequently, the bulk of the British units make a short retreat toward Queenston (1b).

2. Notifying Major General Brown of the termination of offensive action, General Ripley orders the retreat of the American army back to Fort Erie (2–2a), where it arrives around midnight.

3. Following the retreat of the Americans from Chippawa in the late afternoon and the additional movement of the bulk of British units toward Queenston and Fort George (off map), small British detachments, supported by Incorporated Militia and Native allies, advance to the Chippawa River (3). Crossing the river on July 28, the British advance detachments concentrate on the south bank at Chippawa (3a) while the Native allies advance to within sight of Fort Erie (3b) and over the following days engage in harassing raids on the American picket positions.

4. July 31–August 2: The reinforced and resupplied British force advances from its positions at Fort George and Queenston (off map), Lundy's Lane (4), and Chippawa (4a), reaching the ferry dock at Fort Erie (4b) on August 2.

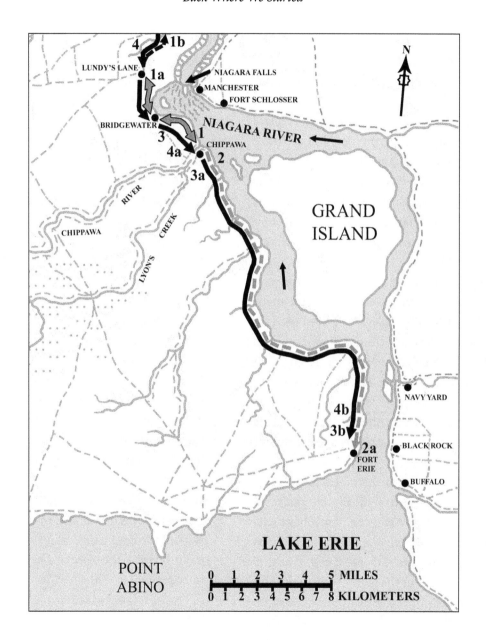

Ripley backed down and agreed to move back to a point near Fort Erie and then decide what should be done next. Setting fire to the small community of Bridgewater Mills, the Americans returned to their camp, while Ripley went to face General Brown and notify him of the decision to cease offensive actions by the army. Furious at this turn of events, but too badly wounded to take back his former command, Brown dismissed Ripley by stating, "Sir, you will do as you please ..."[8] before allowing himself to be shipped out for medical attention at Buffalo.

Although the order to break camp and prepare to march was given, difficulties arose because many of the wagons, which had previously been used for transporting supplies and ammunition, had been filled with wounded men and were already on their way back to Fort Erie. As a result, after allowing the troops a free hand to help themselves to anything they were prepared to carry, the remaining valuable stockpiles of camp equipment, weapons, ammunition, and food were either destroyed or dumped into the Niagara River to prevent them from falling into the hands of the British. Finally, around three in the afternoon, the American army began its retreat to Fort Erie. During the march, discussions between Ripley and his staff produced a further division of opinion over the issue of where the best location to establish a defensive position was. In the end, General Ripley was forced to overrule his engineers' strong recommendations for securing the river crossing opposite Black Rock and instead selected the fort itself as the centre of the American defensive efforts.

> General Ripley ... determined, not without much opposition from the ablest counsellors of the Army to retire upon Fort Erie, and take position, either at that place or on the heights opposite Black-rock. The Engineers opposing every part of this movement were understood, of course, to prefer the latter to the former. The final question seems to have been settled on the march.... By abandoning his position, he put the Army, its artillery, all its supplies, and the whole Niagara frontier into the power of the enemy; but fortunately... Drummond out blundered him and failed to avail himself of any of the advantages thus offered to him.... The General was personally brave ... but ... his flight from Chippawa, had shaken the confidence of all the principal officers of the Army in his capacity to command in Chief ...
>
> — Lieutenant Douglass[9]

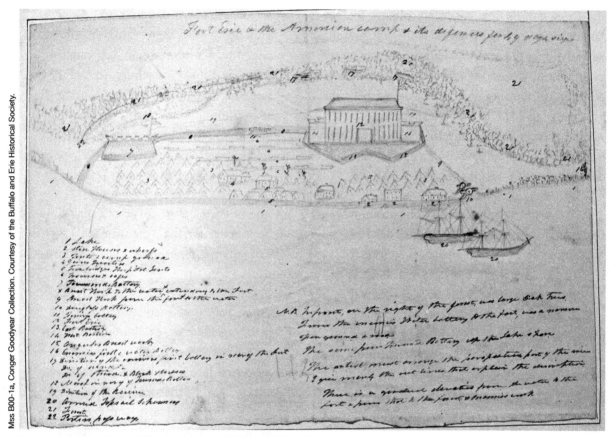

A contemporary view of the American positions at Fort Erie during the siege.

Shortly before midnight on the twenty-sixth, the troops arrived at Fort Erie and, according to Lieutenant Douglass, "bivouacked for the night. The men slept where and how they could; and, too tired to be over fastidious, I stretched myself upon the first camp waggon I saw … which proved to have been loaded with pickaxes, spades, crowbars, and various other tools and mining implements …"[10] — items that were to prove vital to the American war effort in the next few weeks.

To some of the surviving officers of the American force on the Niagara, while going on the defensive after the battle of Lundy's Lane was a campaign necessity, the retreat from the good defensive position at Chippawa smacked of defeatism at the time and resulted in the subsequent misfortunes that were to occur. Consequently, later accounts by various individuals, from Brown down, sought to shift the blame for this situation onto General Ripley.

> The Army, abandoned its strong position behind the Chippawa, and after destroying a part of its stores, fell back, or rather fled, to the ferry opposite Black Rock, but a short distance below Fort Erie and Genl. Ripley, but for the opposition made ... would have crossed to the American shore.... Had the enemy availed himself of this blunder, not a man of our Army could have escaped ...
>
> — Major Jesup[11]

> Change in command, not infrequently, produces change in the course of action.... Had the command descended but one step [to Scott], no one would have apprehended any change in the character of the Campaign.... Had it descended three steps, to General P.B. Porter,

very nearly the same result would apply, with nearly the same force. In either case, the question would be, whether the army should be reinforced, on the battle-ground at the Falls, or occupy its position at Chippawa.... In the new state of things, however, a more cautious policy was adopted ..."

— Lieutenant Douglass[12]

General Porter even advocated that it would have been better for the American war effort if it had been Ripley and not Brown and Scott that was wounded!

> Our victory was complete, but alas, this victory gained by exhibitions of bravery never surpassed in this country was converted into a defeat by a precipitate retreat, leaving the dead, the wounded and captured artillery, and our hard earned honor to the enemy. I entered my remonstrance against this measure and I confess at the time I almost wished that fate had swept another general from the combat ..."
>
> — General Porter to Governor Tompkins, July 29, 1814[13]

In reporting the course of events at Lundy's Lane to Washington a few days later, General Brown created further problems when his official report belittled Ripley's contributions and effectively impugned the commanders of the First and Twenty-Third Infantry Regiments for their "failure" to match the actions of the Twenty-First Regiment in storming the hill. In addition, because the wounded General Scott failed to submit any official report on the actions of the First Brigade, Brown's report only commended Winfield Scott and Major Jesup for their actions in the battle, while virtually ignoring the contributions of Major Leavenworth's (Ninth), Colonel Brady's (Twenty-Second), and Major McNeil's (Eleventh) regiments. This created a backlash of resentment in the First Brigade against both General Brown and General Scott, who were considered to have deliberately sought to garner all the credit themselves.

For their part, having re-established their defensive position on the hilltop, the British remained on the alert throughout the afternoon of July 26 and completed the task of dealing with the remaining bodies from both armies. By late afternoon, the situation eased when reports indicated the Americans were dismantling their camp and retiring to the south, leaving the Chippawa open for occupation. Had Drummond not been wounded (the musket ball was still lodged in his neck) or his troops suffered less from the previous night's action, then it is probable that the British would have actively harassed the retreating Americans, or at the very least advanced to secure the Chippawa crossing. Instead, Drummond issued orders that only elements of the Natives and light troops were to advance on Chippawa, while the remainder of his diminished force was to retire on Queenston to regroup and await reinforcements. For this action, Drummond was later, like Ripley, subjected to the criticism of his own subordinates:

> General Drummond commanded in the action [at Lundy's Lane], but I am sorry to say I could not then or now observe the smallest appearance of generalship. I fear he has got his command, like many others, from the interest of friends, not from his own merit ..."
>
> — Colonel Hercules Scott, 103rd Regiment, August 12, 1814[14]

Despite dismissing the effects of his wound in a letter to his wife, Drummond's injury was serious enough to require surgery the following day, further incapacitating the general. This left the army without an overall commander, and only Norton's Native warriors, accompanied by a detachment of the 19th Light Dragoons and some companies of the Incorporated Militia, remained in contact with the enemy.

Finding that the Americans had destroyed the bridge that crossed the Chippawa River, the advance force encamped until early on July 28, when they crossed to the south bank and established a defensive perimeter. From here, the Natives continued to move down the treeline parallel to the riverbank road, passing the former site of the American camp and the mounds indicating the graves of those who fell at the battle of Chippawa before setting up their own defensive position. Shortly thereafter, they were approached by emissaries from the Americans, ostensibly asking for an exchange of prisoners. Suspicious that this request was a diversion in order to allow the enemy officers to assess the positions and strengths of the British force, Norton forwarded the messages by his own courier and kept the Americans in place, chatting casually until a negative response came from the British commander that sent the American delegation back to Fort Erie empty-handed. Norton's warriors then maintained an aggressive presence in the area, seizing some of the American boats moored at the Black Rock ferry point and reporting on the progress of strengthening the encampment at Fort Erie until the first units of the British force finally approached on August 2.

During this same intermission, when the two armies were effectively separated, much had occurred in the American camp. Having reached Fort Erie, General Ripley was still not convinced that a defence on the Canadian side of the river was viable. He therefore crossed to Buffalo on July 27 and requested General Brown's support for the evacuation of the army from the west bank. To say that Brown was shocked would be an understatement, as he had only shortly before been notified "that the Army had fallen back in haste and was there near him on the opposite side of the strait ..."[15]

Since the eve of the invasion, Brown's confidence in Ripley had been steadily eroding, to the point that he had already decided to replace him as the commander of the army by sending orders for General Gaines to travel post-haste from Sackets Harbor to take over command. Brown later justified this action by claiming:

General Brown had entertained no doubt of the intelligence or bravery of Genl. Ripley, nor had he ever expressed any. — In consequence however of the events of the night of the 25th and more especially, of the morning of the 26th, his confidence in him as a commander was sensibly diminished. The General believed that he dreaded responsibility more than danger. — In short, that he had a greater share of physical than of moral courage.... A courier was dispatched without loss of time, to Genl. Gaines, ordering him to take the command of the gallant remains of the Army of Niagara ...

— General Brown[16]

However, Ripley's latest request proved to be the final straw for Brown. In response, he verbally flayed Ripley for his attitude and sent him packing with verbal instructions to maintain his position at Fort Erie. Ripley, in turn, demanded — and subsequently received — written instructions to that effect:

Headquarters, Buffalo, 27 July 1814, Sir, All the sick and wounded & the surplus baggage will be immediately removed to this place; Those men who are sound and able to fight will encamp at Fort Erie so as to defend that post and at the same time, hold the ferry below until the wounded, sick, and surplus baggage have crossed ...[17]

Ripley was reported to have openly stated "that he would not be responsible for the Army if it remained in Canada ..."[18] Nonetheless, Ripley returned to Fort Erie and issued the orders to commence improving the defences of the fort in preparation for the enemy's arrival. He also penned a letter to the secretary of war, John Armstrong, demanding that a Court of Inquiry be held over the incidents surrounding the battle at Lundy's Lane and Brown's criticisms of Ripley's leadership and actions during the retreat. Relations between Brown and Ripley were beyond repair, and once he heard from Armstrong about Ripley's demand for a Court of Inquiry, Brown's subsequent reports and letters regularly denigrated Ripley and his command judgments.

Things were not much better with General Porter. As a prominent member of the "War Hawks" in the pre-war period, and having been active throughout virtually all of the actions on the Niagara in 1813, Porter already harboured resentment over the way he and his militia had been treated as "inferior" troops during this 1814 campaign. Consequently, upon hearing of Brown's determination to supersede Ripley with an "outsider," instead of devolving the responsibility on him, Porter considered himself fully justified in submitting his resignation from the army.

Our Canadian campaign seems drawing to a close, or must, at any rate be suspended for want of reinforcements. After a month spent in marching and countermarching, we have got back to the point from which we set out, much impaired in strength but I hope not disheartened.... But it is certain that no Militia general is to gain any military fame while united to a regular force and commanded by their officers. The purpose of this letter is to request that I may be permitted to retire from the service, for in truth, the volunteer force is now so small as not to warrant a Brigadier's command. You will know how greatly my expectations have been disappointed in relation to this command. I expected that the force would … assert its equal rights and privileges with the regular troops, and not be what an inferior militia force will always be, the tools and drudges of the regular troops. As regard myself, I did expect too, that I would not be lower than second in command, and that if the fortune of war should dispose of the first, I might take my chance to fill his place. But all hopes of such an event have vanished, for altho' I am now second in command, another Brigadier has been sent for to Sackett's Harbor. In short I have been brigadiered till I am quite satisfied …"

— General Porter to Governor Tompkins, July 29, 1814[19]

In response, Brown was quick to decline Porter's resignation and issued yet another series of glowing reports on the general and his militia command in an effort to salve that officer's pride. The continued existence of the American army on the Niagara now hung in the balance and if the British had attacked, they could probably have swept the Americans out of the peninsula with relatively little effort or additional loss. However, no such attack took place and once the command was given to extend the fortifications at Fort Erie, the entire army set to work at a feverish pace to erect a line of batteries and palisades that would hold the British at bay.

After it fell into our hands, on the third of July, and until the twenty-sixth, when we returned to it, the American garrison had been engaged in improving and completing its defences, as a mere fort; but of course, without any idea of the neighbouring ground being occupied by the army at large; nor had any works with reference to such an occupancy, been laid out or contemplated in the labors of the garrison. The Fort Erie of the siege …was rather an entrenched camp, having the proper fort, indeed, for one of its strong points, but extending for more than half a mile from it, along

Above: The interior courtyard of the restored historic site of Fort Erie today, looking from the western gun platform toward the northern demi-bastion.

Left: The ditch, northern demi-bastion, and northern "mess-house" barracks of the restored historic site of Fort Erie, 2013. Reconstructed from a derelict shell of masonry and earthworks between 1937 and 1939, today Fort Erie is maintained by the Niagara Parks Commission. The flying of the 1814 U.S. flag in this image commemorates the American occupation in 1814 and is part of the annual Living History re-enactment that takes place at this location at the beginning of August.

the lakeshore, with numerous other redoubts and batteries; and embracing an area sufficient for the accommodation of two or three thousand men.... On the twenty-eighth and following days of the month ... the works of intrenchment

were commenced. The ground plan of a battery, for the extreme right of the position, was traced on the lime kiln occupied by the Sappers and Miners, and immediately commenced by them. Another, of larger dimensions and in bolder relief, was laid out, on Snake-hill, on the extreme left; and a fatigue party, of several hundred men, was placed under my directions for its construction. The intermediate ground, between Snake-hill and the fort, was, at the same time, laid out in a system of breastworks and batteries, to be thrown up by the Regimental fatigue parties and Artillery, each in front of its respective Regiment and Corps …

— Lieutenant Douglass[20]

By the time the first British regiments marched into range of Fort Erie on August 2, they found to their chagrin that they were not going to attack the small, half-dilapidated set of barracks and bastions that they had left, but an entire fortified encampment, nearly half a mile long, surrounded by an expanding line of ditches and abattis, palisades and bastions, fully equipped with cannon and backed by troops with well-established fields of fire. The siege of Fort Erie was about to begin, the story of which will be told as part of the final book of this series, *The Ashes of War.*

NOTES

A star indicates the note refers to a sidebar

ABBREVIATIONS:

LAC: Library and Archives Canada

AOO: Archives of Ontario

CRDH: Ernest Cruikshank, *The Documentary History of the Campaigns upon the Niagara Frontier 1812–1814*, 9 Volumes (Welland, ON: Tribune Press, 1896–1908)

CGMC: Buffalo and Erie County Historical Society Archives, B00-11, A. Conger Goodyear War of 1812 Manuscripts, 1779–1862

SBD1812:   William C.H. Wood, *Select British Documents of the War of 1812*, 3 Volumes (Toronto: Champlain Society of Canada, 1920)

CHAPTER 1: INTRODUCTION

*1.   CRDH, Vol. 2, 408. In later years, the actual strength of the American invasion force became a matter of contention between several of the principal participants, as they gave testimonies at the official inquiries and courts martial dealing with the events that subsequently took place during this campaign. Many later accounts used the figures marked * in the sidebar in order to assess the initial size of the invasion force at around three thousand or less. However, this reference was derived from a document dated June 30, 1814, and was a column in the official American regimental rolls that only referred to those officers, non-commissioned officers, and rank and file actually present and on parade on that day.

As a result, it seriously underestimated the real size of the subsequent American invasion force, as it did not include those troops otherwise assigned for that day's guard pickets, camp duties and fatigues, those on detached duties away from the camp, and those reported as sick. In addition, it ignored all headquarters staff, commissariat, and supply staff, musicians, pioneers, surgeons, non-combatant troops, et cetera.

The column giving the total personnel figures of this list do include these additional numbers, but make no breakdown by rank or service/duty. Since virtually all of these latter individuals would have been recalled from their designated duties to participate in the invasion, the initial actual invasion force entering Upper Canada on June 3, 1814, should probably be assessed at somewhere around five thousand men, which was then reinforced by the arrival of the bulk of General Porter's Third Brigade and other regular and militia regiments during the following two weeks.

This assessment is supported by the fact that on May 30, 1814, Brown forwarded a letter to Secretary of War Armstrong, stating, " General Porter has ... from a thousand to twelve hundred [militia] engaged ... if we are to be delayed until this force is in condition to act, much time will, I fear be wasted. With your approval I shall not hesitate to cross ... with my four thousand Regulars, but it would no doubt be desirable to have a greater force, if a greater could be promptly assembled" (Ernest Cruikshank, *Documents Relating to the Invasion of the Niagara Peninsula by the United States Army, Commanded by General Jacob Brown in July and August 1814*. In *The Niagara Historical Society Papers*, No. 33, 1921), followed by a similar letter on June 3, "I believe that from four to five hundred Native warriors may be induced to join us.... I shall consider it my duty to pass into the enemies country the moment I find at my command five thousand Regulars." (*Ibid.*) In return, Armstrong wrote to Brown on June 9, "Sir ... the difference between your effective strength and aggregate numbers is so great as to render it proper that you should immediately despatch an officer to call in and march to their regiments respectfully all absentees of the Line coming within the meaning of this order and are not, in any case, to be exempted from this order ..." (*Ibid.*)

*2. LAC, RG8-I: British Military and Naval Records, 1757–1903, Vol. 1, 77–79.

CHAPTER 2: MANOEUVRING FOR ADVANTAGE: THE NIAGARA FRONTIER, JULY 6–23, 1814

1. SBD1812, Vol. 3, Part 1, 115–16; CRDH Vol.1, 32.
2. *Ibid.*
3. Diary of Ensign Andrew Wharffe, Burton Historical Library, Detroit, MI (entry dated for July 8, 1814).
4. Henry Ruttan, *Reminiscences of the Hon. Henry Ruttan*, in *Loyalist Narratives from Upper Canada* (Toronto: Champlain Society, 1946); AAO, Henry Ruttan Papers, MS74.R5.
5. *Ibid.*
6. *Ibid.*
7. *Ibid.*
8. LAC, MG24, I3: Archibald McLean Papers, Vol. 9.
9. David B. Douglass, "An Original Narrative of the Niagara Campaign in 1814," in *The Historical Magazine*. Vol. II, Third Series (1873) (Buffalo and Erie County Historical Society), 10–11.
10. CGMC, Vol. 5 (Orderly Book of General Jacob Brown, April–August 1814).
11. *Ibid.*
*12. LAC, RG8-I: British Military and Naval Records, 1757–1903, Vol. 1709, 87.
13. LAC, RG8-I: British Military and Naval Records, 1757–1903, Vol. 387, 146.
14. LAC, MG24, I3: Archibald McLean Papers, Vol. 9.
15. CRDH, Vol. 1, 36.
16. CRDH, Vol. 1, 57–58.
17. CRDH, Vol. 1, 59.
18. LAC, MG19, A39: Duncan Clark Papers, Vol. 3, 261.
19. CRDH, Vol. 1, 60.
*20. LAC, MG19, A39: Duncan Clark Papers, Vol. 3, 259.
21. CRDH, Vol. 1, 64 and CGMC, Vol. 5 (Orderly Book of General Jacob Brown, April–August 1814).
22. CRDH, Vol. 1, 68–69.
23. CRDH, Vol. 1, 73.
24. CRDH, Vol. 1, 76–77.
25. CGMC, Vol. 14. Major Thomas S. Jesup, *Memoir of Events on the Niagara Frontier, 1814*: 9

26. CGMC, Vol. 3 General Jacob Brown, *Memorandum of Occurrences Attending the Campaign on the Niagara, 1814.*
27. CRDH, Vol. 2, 416–17.
28. CRDH, Vol. 1, 84.
29. LAC, RG8-I: British Military and Naval Records, 1757–1903, Vol. 684, 169.

CHAPTER 3: THE ROADS TO BATTLE, JULY 24–25, 1814

*1. CGMC, Vol. 3, General Jacob Brown, *Memorandum of Occurrences Attending the Campaign on the Niagara, 1814*; E.A. Ripley, *Facts Relative to the Campaign on the Niagara in 1814* (Boston, self-published, 1815). The accurate calculation of American troop numbers involved in this battle are almost impossible to achieve, as different commanders, seeking to present their own best possible defence in response to the criticism that arose from the outcome of the battle, chose to base their calculations upon a widely varying set of criteria and source data. Primary examples of this were Winfield Scott's and Ripley's decisions to make their calculations of participants in the fighting based upon the exclusion of all ranks above the rank and file (thus ignoring the sergeants and officers), as well as omitting all support personnel, non-combatants, and those listed as on separate duties or sick.
*2. CRDH Vol. 1, 50.

CHAPTER 4: FIRST CONTACT AND THE RACE FOR THE HILLTOP

1. David B. Douglass, "An Original Narrative of the Niagara Campaign in 1814," in *The Historical Magazine*, Vol. II, Third Series (1873) (Buffalo and Erie County Historical Society), 13.
2. Winfield Scott, *Memoirs of Lieut. General Scott* (Sheldon & Co., 1864), 139.
3. LAC, MG19, A39: Duncan Clark Papers, Vol. 3.
4. John Kilborn, "Accounts of the War of 1812," in T.W.H. Leavitt, *A History of Leeds and Grenville Counties from 1749 to 1879* (Brockville, ON: 1879), 70.
5. CGMC, Vol. 15.
6. James Wilkinson, *Memoirs of My Own Times* (Philadelphia: Abraham Small, 1816), Vol. 1, 687.

CHAPTER 5: THE BATTLE OF LUNDY'S LANE, JULY 25, 1814: STAND AND FIGHT

1. LAC, MG19, A39: Duncan Clark Papers, Vol. 1.
2. John Kilborn, "Accounts of the War of 1812," in T.W.H. Leavitt, *A History of Leeds and Grenville Counties from 1749 to 1879* (Brockville: 1879), 70.
3. *Ibid.*
4. William Dunlop, *Tiger Dunlop's Upper Canada* (Carleton University, 1967).
5. John Kilborn, "Accounts of the War of 1812," in T.W.H. Leavitt, *A History of Leeds and Grenville Counties from 1749 to 1879* (Brockville: 1879), 7.
6. LAC, MG19, A39: Duncan Clark Papers, Vol. 1.
7. Diary of Ensign Andrew Warffe, Burton Historical Library, Detroit, MI. Entry dated for July 25, 1814.
8. John Kilborn, "Accounts of the War of 1812," in T.W.H. Leavitt, *A History of Leeds and Grenville Counties from 1749 to 1879* (Brockville, 1879), 70.
9. *Ibid.*
10. James Wilkinson, *Memoirs of my Own Times* (Philadelphia, Abraham Small, 1816), Vol. 1, 688.

CHAPTER 6: THE GUNS MUST BE TAKEN!

1. Brigadier General Ripley's report on Lundy's Lane, 1812 manuscript collection, Lilly Library, Indiana University.
2. *Ibid.*
3. *Testimony of Captain Symes at Lieutenant Colonel Nicholas' Court Martial*, 1812 manuscript collection, Lilly Library, Indiana University.

4. CGMC, Vol. 3, General Jacob Brown, *Memorandum of Occurrences Attending the Campaign on the Niagara, 1814.*

5. *Ibid.*

6. CGMC, Vol. 14, Thomas S. Jesup, *Memoir of Events on the Niagara Frontier, 1814*: 15.

7. CGMC, Vol. 3, General Jacob Brown, *Memorandum of Occurrences Attending the Campaign on the Niagara, 1814*; E.A. Ripley, *Facts Relative to the Campaign on the Niagara in 1814* (Boston, self-published, 1815), 13.

8. David B. Douglass, "An Original Narrative of the Niagara Campaign in 1814," in *The Historical Magazine*, Vol. II, Third Series, 1873 (Buffalo and Erie County Historical Society), 17.

9. CGMC, Vol. 3, General Jacob Brown, *Memorandum of Occurrences Attending the Campaign on the Niagara, 1814*: 20.

10. *Ibid.*, 20–21.

11. *Ibid.*, 21.

12. Henry Ruttan, *Reminiscences of the Hon. Henry Ruttan*, in *Loyalist Narratives from Upper Canada* (Toronto: Champlain Society, 1946).

13. *Ibid.*

14. LAC, RG9.IB1: Pre-Confederation Records, Military, Lampman, Vol. 3.

CHAPTER 7: A CRUCIBLE OF FIRE: THE BRITISH COUNTERATTACKS

1. LAC, MG19, A39: Duncan Clark Papers, Vol. 1.

2. CGMC, Vol. 3: General Jacob Brown, *Memorandum of Occurrences Attending the Campaign on the Niagara, 1814.*

3. LAC, MG19, A39: Duncan Clark Papers, Vol. 1.

4. CGMC, Vol. 14: Thomas S. Jesup, *Memoir of Events on the Niagara Frontier, 1814*: 16.

5. *Ibid.*

6. LAC, MG19, A39: Duncan Clark Papers, Vol. 1.

7. CGMC, Vol. 3: General Jacob Brown, *Memorandum of Occurrences Attending the Campaign on the Niagara, 1814.*

8. CGMC, Vol. 15.

9. James Wilkinson, *Memoirs of My Own Times* (Philadelphia: Abraham Small, 1816), Vol. 1, 712.

10. *Ibid.*

11. CGMC, Vol. 3: General Jacob Brown, *Memorandum of Occurrences Attending the Campaign on the Niagara, 1814.*

12. CRDH, Vol.2, 376.

13. CGMC, Vol. 3: General Jacob Brown, *Memorandum of Occurrences Attending the Campaign on the Niagara, 1814.*

14. E.A. Ripley, *Facts Relative to the Campaign on the Niagara in 1814* (Boston, self-published, 1815), 44.

15. *Ibid.*

16. Donald Graves (ed.), *Merry Hearts Make Light Days: The War of 1812 Journal of Lieutenant John Le Couteur, 104th Foot* (Ottawa: Carleton University Press, 1993), 175–76.

*17. LAC, RG8-I: British Military and Naval Records, 1757–1903, Vol. 695, 233; Vol. 1219, 265.

18. CRDH, Vol. 2, 420–21. It is an unfortunate fact that the accurate calculation of American troop numbers involved and casualties suffered in this battle have proved almost impossible to assess. This is because Generals Brown, Scott, Ripley, and Porter, each seeking to present their own best possible defence in response to the criticism that arose from the outcome of the battle, chose to base their calculations upon a widely varying and sometimes contradictory series of criteria and data sources. For example, the initial figures for casualties of the First Brigade, as well as the combined force of the Second and Third Brigades shown in this reference, are taken from the report made by General Winfield Scott. The bracketed numbers () are those issued within an official U.S. report dated July 31, 1814. In comparison, Colonel Miller, in a post-battle letter to his wife, recorded that his command (the Twenty-First Regiment, Second Brigade) alone suffered 126 casualties killed, wounded, and missing from an initial complement of 432 (all ranks). While Leavenworth's account for the Ninth Regiment (First Brigade) listed a loss of 128 (all ranks) in this battle and a post-battle effective strength on the morning of July 26 of only 64 men from a pre-battle estimated complement of around 180–200 (all ranks).

Consequently, despite two decades of number crunching, this author has to admit that the actual numbers still remain something of a mystery of history.

19. James Wilkinson, *Memoirs of My Own Times* (Philadelphia: Abraham Small, 1816), Vol. 1, 684.
20. *Ibid.*, 717.

CHAPTER 8: BACK WHERE WE STARTED

1. LAC, MG19, A39: Duncan Clark Papers, Vol. 1.
2. J. Lampman, "Reminiscences of the War," in *Welland County Historical Society, Papers and Records*, Vol. 3 (1927); LAC, RG9.IB1: Pre-Confederation Records, Military, Lampman, Vol. 3.
3. James Wilkinson, *Memoirs of My Own Times* (Philadelphia: Abraham Small, 1816), Vol. 1, Appendix IX; E.A. Ripley, *Facts Relative to the Campaign on the Niagara in 1814* (Boston: self-published, 1815), 27.
4. CGMC, Vol. 3: General Jacob Brown, *Memorandum of Occurrences Attending the Campaign on the Niagara, 1814.*
5. James Wilkinson, *Memoirs of My Own Times* (Philadelphia: Abraham Small, 1816), Vol. 1, Appendix IX; E.A. Ripley, *Facts Relative to the Campaign on the Niagara in 1814* (Boston: self-published, 1815), 20.
6. CGMC, Vol. 3: General Jacob Brown, *Memorandum of Occurrences Attending the Campaign on the Niagara, 1814.*
7. E.A. Ripley, *Facts Relative to the Campaign on the Niagara in 1814* (Boston: self-published, 1815), 35.
8. CGMC, Vol. 3, General Jacob Brown, *Memorandum of Occurrences Attending the Campaign on the Niagara, 1814.*
9. David B. Douglass, "An Original Narrative of the Niagara Campaign in 1814," in *The Historical Magazine*, Vol. II, Third Series, 1873 (Buffalo and Erie County Historical Society), 22.
10. *Ibid.*
11. CRDH Vol. 2, 473; CGMC, Vol. 14, Thomas S. Jesup, *Memoir of Events on the Niagara Frontier, 1814*, 19.
12. David B. Douglass, "An Original Narrative of the Niagara Campaign in 1814," in *The Historical Magazine*. Vol. II, Third Series, 1873 (Buffalo and Erie County Historical Society), 22.
13. CRDH Vol.1, 101.
14. CRDH Vol.1, 131.
15. CGMC, Vol. 3, General Jacob Brown, *Memorandum of Occurrences Attending the Campaign on the Niagara, 1814.*
16. *Ibid.*
17. *Ibid.*
18. *Ibid.*
19. CRDH Vol.1, 101–02.
20. David B. Douglass, "An Original Narrative of the Niagara Campaign in 1814," in *The Historical Magazine*. Vol. II, Third Series, 1873 (Buffalo and Erie County Historical Society), 23–24.

SELECTED BIBLIOGRAPHY

PRIMARY SOURCES

Archival
1. Library and Archives Canada
    Manuscript Groups (MG)
        MG10A: U.S. Department of State, War of 1812 Records
        MG11 (CO42): British Colonial Office, Original Correspondence, Canada
        MG11 (CO47): Upper Canada Records, 1764–1836, Miscellaneous
        MG13 (WO62): Commissariat Dept., Miscellaneous Records 1809–1814
        MG19, A39: Duncan Clark Papers
        MG24, A9: Sir George Prevost Papers
        MG24, I3: Archibald McLean Papers
    Research Groups (RG)
        RG5-A1: Civil Secretary's Office, Upper Canada Sundries, 1791–1867
        RG8-I: British Military and Naval Records, 1757–1903
        RG9-I: Pre-Confederation Records, Military
        RG10: Indian Department Records
        RG19/E5A: Department of Finance, War of 1812, Losses Board

2. Archives Ontario
        MS35/1: Strachan Papers
        MS74/R5: Merritt Papers
        MS501: Thorburn Papers
        MS58: Band Papers
        MS500: Street Papers
        MS502/B Series: Nelles Papers
        MU2099: A.A. Rapelje Papers
        MU527: Duncan Clark Papers
        MS74.R5: Henry Ruttan Papers

3. Metro Toronto Reference Library
        Hagerman, C.: Journal of Christopher Hagerman
        Prevost Papers, 7 Volumes, S108, Cub 7

4. Detroit Public Library Archives
        Kirby, J.: James Kirby Papers

5. Buffalo and Erie County Historical Society Archives, A. Conger Goodyear: War of 1812 Manuscripts, 1779–1862, Mss. BOO-11. 16 Volumes

6. Burton Historical Library, Detroit, MI, Diary of Ensign Andrew Wharffe

7. Lilly Library, Indiana University, 1812 manuscript collection

Early Secondary Publications

Armstrong, J. *Notices of the War of 1812*. New York: Wiley & Putnam, 1840.

Boyd, J.P. *Documents and Facts Relative to Military Events during the Late War*. Private publication, 1816.

Brackenridge, Henry M. *History of the Late War Between the United States and Great Britain*. Cushing & Jewett, 1817.

Brannan, J. *Official Letters of the Military and Naval Officers of the United States, during the War with Great Britain in the Years 1812, 13, 14, & 15*. Washington City: Way & Gideon, 1823.

Chapin, C. *Chapin's Review of Armstrong's Notices of the War of 1812*. Black Rock, NY: Private publication, 1836.

Congreve, Colonel Sir W. *The Details of the Rocket System, Shewing the Various Applications of This Weapon, Both for Sea and Land Service, and Its Different Uses in the Field and in Sieges*. London: J. Whiting, 1814.

Davis, Paris M. *An Authentick History of the Late War Between the United States and Great Britain*. Ithaca, NY: Mack & Andrus, 1829.

————. *The Four Principal Battles of the Late War Between the United States and Great Britain*. Harrisburg, NY: Jacob Baab, 1832.

Gilleland, J.C. *History of the Late War Between the United States and Great Britain*. Baltimore, MD: Schaeffer & Maund, 1817.

Hitsman, J.M. *History of the American War of Eighteen Hundred and Twelve*. Philadelphia: W. McCarty, 1816.

James, W. *A Full and Correct Account of the Military Occurrences of the Late War Between Great Britain and the United States of America*. London: William James, 1818.

McCarty, W. *History of the American War of 1812*. Philadelphia: William McCarty & Davis, 1817.

Merritt, William Hamilton. *Journal of Events: Principally on the Detroit & Niagara Frontiers during the War of 1812*. St. Catharines, CW: Canada West Historical Society, 1863.

Morgan, J.C. *The Emigrant's Guide, With Recollections of Upper and Lower Canada during the Late War Between the United States of America and Great Britain*. London: Longman, Hurst, Rees, Orme & Brown, 1824.

O'Connor, T. *An Impartial and Correct History of the War Between the United States of America and Great Britain*. Belfast: Joseph Smyth, 1816. Reprint of the John Low edition, New York, 1815.

Official Correspondence with the Department of War Relative to the Military Operations of the American Army Under the Command of Major General Izard of the Northern Frontier of the United States in the Years 1814 and 1815. Philadelphia: Thomas Dobson, 1816.

Perkins, S. *A History of the Political and Military Events of the Late War Between the United States and Great Britain*. New Haven, CT: S. Converse, 1825.

"Proceedings and Debates of the House of Representatives of the United States." 12th Congress, 1st Session (1812). U.S. Government Records.

Ripley, E.A. *Facts Relative to the Campaign on the Niagara in 1814*. Boston: Self-published, 1815.

Sturtevant, I. *Barbarities of the Enemy Exposed in a Report of the Committee of the House of Representatives of the United States*. Worcester, MA: Remark Dunnell, 1814.

Thomson, J.L. *Historical Sketches of the Late War Between the United States and Great Britain*. Philadelphia: Thomas Delsilver, 1816.

Wilkinson, J. *Diagrams and Plans Illustrative of the Principal Battles of the War of 1812*. Philadelphia: Self-published, 1815.

————. *Memoirs of My Own Times*. Philadelphia: Abraham Small, 1816.

SECONDARY SOURCES

Later Secondary Publications

Baylies, N. *Eleazer Wheellock Ripley, of the War of 1812*. Des Moines, IA: Brewster & Co., 1890.

Buell, W. *Military Movements in Eastern Ontario during the War of 1812*. Ontario Historical Society, Papers and Records, Vol. 10 (1913) and Vol. 17 (1919).

Cannon, R. *Historical Record of the 1st or Royal Regiment of Foot*. London, UK: William Clowes & Sons, 1847.

_____. *Historical Record of the Eighth or the King's Regiment of Foot*. London: Harrison & Co., 1844.

Carnochan, Janet. *Reminiscences of Niagara and St. David's*. Niagara Historical Society, Paper No. 20 (1911).

Cruickshank, Ernest. *Campaigns of 1812–1814*. Niagara Historical Society, Paper No. 9 (1902).

_____. *Documents Relating to the Invasion of the Niagara Peninsula by the United States Army, Commanded by General Jacob Brown in July and August 1814*. Niagara Historical Society Papers, No. 33 (1921).

_____. *Letters of 1812 from the Dominion Archives*. Niagara Historical Society, Papers No. 23 (1913).

_____. *A Memoir of Colonel the Honourable James Kerby, His Life in Letters*. Welland County Historical Society, Papers and Records, No. 4 (1931).

Douglass, David B. "An Original Narrative of the Niagara Campaign in 1814." *The Historical Magazine*, Vol. II, Third Series, 1873. Buffalo and Erie County Historical Society.

Edgar M. *Ten Years in Upper Canada in Peace & War, 1805–1815: Being the Ridout Letters with Annotations by Matilda Edgar*. Toronto: William Brigs, 1890.

Family History and Reminiscences of Early Settlers and Recollections of the War of 1812. Niagara Historical Society, Paper No. 28 (1915).

Government of the United States. *Causes of the Failure of the Army on the Northern Frontier*. Report to the House of Representatives, February 2, 1814, 13th Congress, 2nd Session, Military Affairs.

Johnson, Frederick H. *A Guide for Every Visitor to Niagara Falls*. Niagara Falls, ON: Self-published, 1852.

Kearsley, Major J. "The Memoirs of Major John Kearsley: A Michigan Hero from the War of 1812." *Military History Journal* 10 (May 1985). Clement Library, University of Michigan.

Kilborn, John. "Accounts of the War of 1812." In Thaddeus W.H. Leavitt. *History of Leeds and Grenville Counties from 1749 to 1879*. Brockville, ON: Recorder Press, 1879.

Leavitt. T.W.H. *History of Leeds and Grenville Counties from 1749 to 1879*. Brockville, ON: Recorder Press, 1879.

Lossing, Benson. *Pictorial Field Book of the War of 1812*. New York: Harper and Brothers, 1868.

Niagara Historical Society Papers, Numbers 2, 3, 4, 5, 9, 11, 20, 22, 23, 28, 30, 31, 33.

Recollections of the Late Hon. James Crooks. Niagara Historical Society Papers, No. 28 (1916).

"Reminiscences of Arthur Galloway." Ithaca, NY: Cornell University Library.

Reminiscences of Niagara. Niagara Historical Society, Paper No. 11 (1904).

Scott, Winfield. *Memoirs of Lieut. General Scott*. New York: Sheldon & Co., 1864. State Historical Monographs, Historical Literature Collection, Anonymous collection, circa 1850.

Severence, F.H., ed. *Papers Relating to the War of 1812 on the Niagara Frontier*. Buffalo Historical Society Publications, No. 5 (1902).

Warner, Robert I. *Memoirs of Capt. John Lampman and His Wife Mary Secord*. Welland County Historical Society, Papers and Records 3, 126–34 (1927).

Books

Adams, Henry. *History of the United States of America during the Administrations of Madison*. New York: Library of America, 1986. Reprint of original 1891 volumes.

Auchinleck, George. *A History of the War Between Great Britain and the United States of America during the Years*

1812, 1813 & 1814. Toronto: Thomas Maclear, 1853. Reprint by Arms & Armour Press and Pendragon House, 1972.

Babcock, Louis L. *The War of 1812 on the Niagara Frontier, Volume 29.* Buffalo, NY: Buffalo Historical Society Publications, 1927.

Benn, Carl. *The Iroquois in the War of 1812.* Toronto: University of Toronto Press, 1998.

Bingham, Robert. W. *The Cradle of the Queen City: A History of Buffalo to the Incorporation of the City, Volume 31.* Buffalo, NY: Buffalo Historical Society Publications, 1931.

Bowler, R. Arthur, ed. *War Along the Niagara: Essays on the War of 1812 and Its Legacy.* Youngstown, NY: Old Fort Niagara Association, 1991.

Brant, Irving. *The Fourth President: A Life of James Madison.* Indianapolis and New York: The Bobbs Merrill Company, 1970.

Casselman, Alexander C., ed. *Richardson's War of 1812.* Toronto: Historical Publishing Co., 1902. Facsimile edition by Coles Publishing Co., Toronto, 1974.

"Contest for the Command of Lake Ontario in 1812 & 1813." Transactions of the Royal Society of Canada, SEC II, Series III, Vol. X.

Cruikshank, Ernest. *The Documentary History of the Campaigns upon the Niagara Frontier in 1812–1814.* 9 volumes. Welland, ON: Tribune Press, 1896–1908.

Dunlop, William (Tiger). *Tiger Dunlop's Upper Canada.* Ottawa: Carleton University Press, 1967.

Elliott, C. *Winfield Scott: The Soldier and the Man.* Toronto: Macmillan, 1937.

Gardiner, Robert, ed. *The Naval War of 1812.* London, UK: Caxton Publishing Group, 2001.

Gayler, Hugh J., ed. *Niagara's Changing Landscapes.* Ottawa: Carleton University Press, 1994.

Gourlay, Robert. *Statistical Account of Upper Canada Compiled with a View to a Grand System of Emigration.* 2 Volumes. London, UK: Simpkin and Marshall, 1822. Republished by the Social Science Research Council of Canada, S.R. Publishers Ltd., Johnson Reprint Corp, 1966.

Graves, D.E. *Fix Bayonets! A Royal Welch Fusilier at War 1796–1815.* Montreal: Robin Brass Studio, 2006.

_____. *The Battle of Lundy's Lane on the Niagara in 1814.* Baltimore, MD: The Nautical & Aviation Publishing Company of America, 1993.

Graves, D.E., ed. *Merry Hearts Make Light Days: The Journal of Lieutenant John Le Couteur, 104th Foot.* Ottawa: Carleton University Press, 1993.

_____. *Soldiers of 1814: American Enlisted Men's Memoirs of the Niagara Campaign.* Youngstown, NY: Old Fort Niagara Association Inc.; Lawrenceville, NJ: Princeton Academic Press, 1995.

Hitsman, J. Mackay. *The Incredible War of 1812: A Military History.* Toronto: Robin Brass Studio, 1999. Revised edition updated by Donald Graves.

Horsman, R. *The Causes of the War of 1812.* New York: A.S. Barnes and Co., 1962.

Illustrated Historical Atlas of the Counties of Lincoln and Welland. Toronto: H.R. Page, 1876.

Irving, L.H. *Officers of the British Forces in Canada during the War of 1812.* Toronto: Canadian Military Institute, 1908.

Jarvis Papers. Women's Canadian Historical Society of Toronto Papers and Transactions, Transaction No. 5 (1902), 3–9.

Jay, W. *Table of the Killed and Wounded in the War of 1812.* Ithaca, NY: New York State Historical Monographs, Historical Literature Collection, Cornell University Library.

Johnston, Winston. *The Glengarry Light Infantry, 1812–1816: Who Were They and What Did They Do in the War?* Self-published, 2011.

Klinck, Carl F. *Journal of Major John Norton.* Toronto: Champlain Society of Canada, Publication No. 46. 1970.

Mackay, J. *The Incredible War of 1812.* Toronto: University of Toronto, 1965.

_____. *Lords of the Lake: The Naval War on Lake Ontario, 1812–1814.* Toronto: Robin Brass Studio, 1998.

Malcomson, Robert. *A Very Brilliant Affair: The Battle of Queenston Heights, 1812.* Toronto: Robin Brass Studio, 2003.

_____. *Warships of the Great Lakes, 1754–1834.* Rochester, UK: Chatham Publishing, 2001.

Ruttan, Henry. *Reminiscences of the Hon. Henry Ruttan: Loyalist Narratives from Upper Canada.* Toronto: Champlain Society, 1946.

Stagg, J.C.A. *Mr. Madison's War: Politics, Diplomacy, and Warfare in the Early American Republic 1783–1830.* Princeton, NJ: Princeton University Press, 1983.

Stanley, George F.G. *The War of 1812: Land Operations.* Toronto: Macmillan and the Canadian War Museum, 1983.

Wood, William C.H. *Select British Documents of the War of 1812.* 3 Volumes. Toronto: Champlain Society of Canada, 1920.

INDEX

FROM THE SAME SERIES

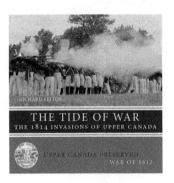

The Tide of War
The 1812 Invasions of Upper Canada
Richard Feltoe

Book four in the Upper Canada Preserved — War of 1812 series. Throughout 1812 and 1813, Upper Canada had been the principle target for a succession of American invasions and attacks. Fortunately they all had been repulsed, but at a high cost in lives and the devastation of property on both sides of the border. By the beginning of 1814, both sides were determined to bring the war to an end with a decisive victory through an escalated commitment of men and military resources.

Continuing the story already detailed in *The Call to Arms*, *The Pendulum of War*, and *The Flames of War*, *The Tide of War* documents the first six months of 1814 and the ongoing fight for the domination and control of Upper Canada.

Available at your favourite bookseller

Visit us at
Dundurn.com | @dundurnpress | Facebook.com/dundurnpress | Pinterest.com/dundurnpress

Printed in the USA
CPSIA information can be obtained
at www.ICGtesting.com
JSHW052017140824
68134JS00027B/2523